❄

Good Mother

Bad Mother

❄

❀

Good Mother Bad Mother

❀

Gina Ford

✓ermilion
LONDON

You painted no Madonnas
On chapel walls in Rome;
But with a touch diviner
You lived one in your home.
You wrote no lofty poems
That critics counted art;
But with a nobler vision,
You lived them in your heart.

You carved no shapeless marble
To some high soul design
But with a finer sculpture
You shaped this soul of mine.
You built no great cathedrals
That centuries applaud;
But with a grace exquisite
Your life cathedraled God.
Had I the gift of Raphael
Or Michelangelo
O what a rare Madonna
My mother's life would show.

Thomas Fessenden

5 7 9 10 8 6

First published in the United Kingdom in 2006 by Vermilion,
an imprint of Ebury Publishing
Random House UK Ltd.
Random House
20 Vauxhall Bridge Road
London SW1V 2SA

Random House Uk Limited Reg. No. 954009
www.randomhouse.co.uk
Papers used by Vermilion are natural, recyclable products
made from wood grown in sustainable forests.

A CIP catalogue record for this book is available from the British Library

ISBN: 9780091954963

The Random House Group Limited supports The Forest Stewardship
Council® (FSC®), the leading international forest-certification organisation.
Our books carrying the FSC label are printed on FSC®-certified paper.
FSC is the only forest-certification scheme supported by the leading
environmental organisations, including Greenpeace. Our
paper procurement policy can be found at
www.randomhouse.co.uk/environment

Typeset by SX Composing DTP, Rayleigh, Essex
Printed and bound in Great Britain by Clays Ltd, St Ives plc

Contents

✻

Contents

Acknowledgements

With thanks to my publisher, Fiona MacIntyre, for recognising the value of this book and giving me the opportunity to send its important message to mothers everywhere. Also to my editor, Imogen Fortes; head of PR, Sarah Bennie; and the rest of the team at Random House for their constant support and hard work in helping me pursue my vision of helping to make the world a better place for mothers everywhere.

Thank you, Emma Todd, for the dedication, energy and encouragement you have given me during the last seven years; Lesley McOwan, my former editor, for believing in this book and for contributing so much to my personal and professional development as a writer; Dawn Fozard for your ongoing support and the excellent job you did in interviewing a great number of the women whose stories are included in this book, and for writing them up with such empathy and understanding. My heartfelt appreciation goes to the women who have taken the time to share with us their unique and touching stories. By doing so they will reassure thousands of mothers that being a mother is not always about getting it right, but simply about doing one's best in the circumstances.

Thank you to all the mothers in my life who befriended me, supported me emotionally and shared their beautiful babies with me after the death of my own mother, in particular Françoise Skelley, Juliette Scott, Helen Sherbourne, Janette Hodgson, Sabrina Masri, Catherine Vaughan William, Terry Moore and Sabine Howard.

My gratitude also goes to the very special people in my life whose love, support and encouragement over the years have helped make me become the person I am today. My family - William Alexander Ford, Andrew and Jean Fair, Robert and Mary Fair, Ann Clough and Sheila Eskdale – who helped give me the strength to deal with my mother's long battle with cancer and the painful years after her death; my friends, Jane Revell and Carla Fodden Flint, who continue to inspire and support me both personally and professionally; Gill Macaulay who has been a wonderful mentor and friend, and who has ensured that I keep the success of CLB in perspective and hold on to my sense of humour!

Sincere thanks to everyone who helped me create Contented baby.com, a wonderful online community that reaches thousands of mothers around the world: Rory Jenkins of Embado for his Internet expertise and technical skills; Russell Nathan of HW Fisher and Paul Hosford of New Media Law for their sound business advice; Frances Howard Brown, a Princess Christian trained nanny of the highest experience, for devoting endless hours to helping me answer the hundreds and thousands of emails we receive each month.

Finally, to my beloved mother and best friend, who I know still watches over me. Thank you for all your amazing wisdom and the very special love and encouragement you always gave me. The answer to the question that your death prevented me from answering lies here in this book. Yes, you were a good mother: you were the best mother any child could wish for.

Introduction

The earliest memory I have of my mother is from when I was less than two years old. We stood on the doorstep of our home in rain and darkness. There was a storm – I remember thunder and lightning – and my father was in the doorway against the light, looking at us. My mother was trying to hold my coat together to protect me from the rain. 'Please,' she begged, 'the baby doesn't have any buttons on her raincoat. She'll get cold.' But he closed the door on us and left us there.

The last memory I have of my mother is visiting her in her hospital bed. For five long years, she had fought against the aggressive lung cancer that had ravaged her body. The debilitating effects of her treatment, the exhausting years of chemotherapy and radiotherapy, had taken their toll, and she was now clinging on to life with the aid of oxygen 24/7 and a permanent morphine drip to help reduce the pain. Now, she was nearing the end and we knew that there was little more that could be done for her. My job as a maternity nurse took me all over the world, working for various clients, but I always came back to her, to see how she was and do what I could for her. We had been through so much together. When I saw her that final time she was so very weak and ill but could still manage a faint smile through the oxygen mask when I entered the room. On this occasion, I told her a lie. I told her that I had a slight cold and because of this I couldn't go too near her, in case of infection. It wasn't true. I knew that if I touched her, even for a moment, I would break down completely and beg her not to die, not to leave me. But there was nothing I could do, or she could do, to prevent it. I was heartbroken – I couldn't go near her, to hug my mother, even though she was dying.

My mother told me to go back to the hotel I was staying at and work on my book. I was writing the first of my childcare books at the time and the deadline for delivering it to the publisher was approaching. I said, 'No, no, I'll stay' and I usually did stay with her, camping down in her room – but my mother insisted, and I let her persuade me to leave. Before I went, she reached out and stroked my wrist, with her warm, comforting touch, and said, 'I love you, honey, you're the world to me, you've been my rock. Now go and finish your book.' Those were her last words to me. She died during the early hours on 10 November 1998.

Between those two memories lies a lifetime, or rather two lifetimes intertwined – mine and hers. The complex, strange and wonderful relationship between a mother and a child was made more intense by the fact that for huge chunks of our lives we only had each other. She loved me deeply and did more for me than I can ever imagine – and I, in return, loved her. Her death left me bereft in a way I hadn't imagined possible. The day after she died, I sat alone in her bedroom. It was a beautiful room, decorated in her favourite colours of lemon and white. She had always loved pretty things, and the room was just as she liked it, with the soft, plump pillows on the bed and the curtains framing the wonderful view of the country-side. I looked out at the scene before me: the rolling cornfields and hills in the distance, with the bluest of skies above; the trees and grass and hedges, all the infinite varieties of green. My mother had loved this view – she used to say, 'Gina, isn't it amazing how many different shades of green there are?' – and we would lie together on the bed, gazing out of the window at the view, talking and laughing. It seemed wrong that the view should remain, that the weather should be so beautiful, when my mother was dead and I had no idea how I would carry on.

The room was full of black bin bags, each one stuffed with my mother's possessions. She had kept everything; there were mementoes of my childhood going back to my earliest days, when I was just learning to read and write. Everything I'd ever written, every card I'd ever sent her, she'd kept. Now I stared at those overflowing bags and was helpless in front of the remnants of my mother's life. How could I decide what to throw away and what to keep? How could I even begin to know how to encapsulate her life from so many bits of paper, so many worn clothes: how could I preserve the essence of her? I had no idea. The bin bags, with their black, suffocating, artificial plastic, seemed like evil things, a terrible contrast to the air and light and growth and life I could see through the window above them.

I felt as though my heart were breaking. And it wasn't only that my mother had died. My aunt had told me that, on her deathbed, my mother had asked her a question – a question that cut me to the quick and caused me such pain, I could feel it like a physical ache. She had said to my aunt, 'Was I a good mother?'

The fact that she could have died not knowing the answer to

this question, the fact that she had asked it at all, was agonising. Of course she was a good mother – she was *my* mother. She wasn't perfect but she'd loved me beyond anything else in the world. I couldn't understand why she had said it and whether that meant that she hadn't really known that I loved her so very much. This question still causes me great pain when I think of it. And yet . . . in the course of my long experience as a maternity nurse and childcare consultant, I've had many, many mothers come to me, desperate and needy, berating themselves because they don't feel they are the ideal mother that they want so terribly to be. They come to me and say, 'Gina, am I a good mother?' They need so much to hear that they are good mothers, because it is something that they can never tell themselves, and never quite believe.

That is why I came to write this book. Now more than ever, as increasing numbers of mothers work, people are questioning what makes a good mother and trying to find an answer. There are theories of childcare, criticisms of women who leave the home, criticisms of women who stay there, of women who care too much and women who don't care enough. As if mothers weren't hard enough on themselves. It is a question that's been asked throughout the ages and remains one of society's biggest preoccupations: how do we raise the next generation properly? And how do mothers cope with this extraordinary responsibility? Among all the criticism and blame, we sometimes forget to praise. We sometimes forget that loving her child is the first and most important thing a mother can do.

Am I a good mother? Or a bad mother? Or am I just myself, flawed but trying to do the best I can? Every mother asks herself these questions. Every child has a relationship with its mother, even if it is cut short by death or adoption. These questions apply to us all and it seems that now, more than ever, we are desperate for the answers. This book is the way that I try to answer my mother and all the other mothers out there who doubt themselves.

Alongside my own attempts at finding an answer, I wanted to include the voices of many mothers in this book in order to show each and every woman reading it that she is not alone in her doubts and her fears. I am indebted to them for sharing their stories with me and I hope that by allowing their voices to be heard, the book provides the comfort and reassurance sought by so many women. This book is about today's mothers but also about yesterday's mothers and tomorrow's mothers.

I recently found a wonderful memoir of motherhood by Anne Enright entitled *Making Babies: Stumbling into Motherhood.* As I spoke to many women during the research for this book, I realised that every single story was of interest and importance. I concur entirely with Enright when she writes: 'A dull mother? There is no such thing. It is odd that, as a group, mothers are seen as a lardy wodge of nothing much; of worry and love and fret and banality. As individuals, we are *everything.*'

And indeed you are.

Gina Ford
Edinburgh, October 2005

Chapter 1

❉

What is
a Good
Mother?

❉

I was at a party several years ago when a woman came up to me. She introduced herself then blurted out: 'You're that woman who writes those routines, well I don't have any routine for my baby, he sleeps with us and I am feeding him on demand.' I took a sip of my champagne and smiled at her. 'I suppose you think I'm a bad mother,' she continued. I assured her that this was not the case at all but she pursued me round that party for the next half-hour, insisting I label her a bad mother who was damaging her baby. Much to her disappointment, I flatly refused to do this.

I suppose it must have stuck with me though, because a little while after that party, I recalled a moment from my childhood. Aged eight years old, I had stamped my foot at my mother, thrown a full-blown tantrum and yelled at the top of my voice, 'I want a *real* mummy!' My mother had said, 'Georgina, what do you mean? *I'm* a real mummy. I'm *your* mummy.'

Looking back, I realise that my mother was gobsmacked

and pretty hurt by my outburst, but I was hopping mad with her. I couldn't understand why she didn't see what I meant; she seemed unaware that to me she was 'different'. It was not what she did, but the way she did it. She cooked and cared for me, but not in the way the homely looking mothers at the school gates managed their lives. Those mothers had big bosoms, bare faces and flowery aprons, and they kept well-ordered homes filled with fresh baking and neatly stacked laundry. By contrast, my mother resembled a glossy fashion plate. She loved high heels and black pencil skirts. She wore dressy coats and little hats, carried neat handbags and always had perfect make-up. 'Here comes Lady Muck,' the other mothers would snipe at the school gates. I was dubbed Madame Muck! Our home was a madhouse at times. The baker's van came twice a week. There was always one day of the week when we'd run out of money. My mother still wanted her buns though, so she'd leave the order stuck firmly on the front door, promising to pay the baker on Friday. Then we'd hide under the stairs until he'd gone. Afterwards, we'd retrieve the buns from the doorstep, scoff them with loads of lemonade, put the radio on top volume and dance round the house together.

Of course, I understand a lot more now than I did at the age of eight, and the things that made my mother different are the things I am most grateful for and treasure about her now. She was proud of standing out from the crowd and I know now that she had ambitions for me that exceeded those of the other mothers in our community. Through always being true to herself, she taught me more than she would have, had she tried to emulate the other women. She used to tell me, 'Gina, you must always march to the beat of your own drum. Even if that means you march alone.' Her strong sense of right and wrong was instilled in me from an early age. She was completely dedicated to my welfare and had been since my father left us when I was two years old. Now I can understand how she struggled, but also why one of the reasons she didn't behave like other mothers was because she had no female role model. Her own mother died when she was eight years old and my grandfather brought her up. At eight, she was expected to cook and clean and consequently, when I was eight, she expected me to carry out similar chores, which the other mothers criticised her for. But my mother didn't expect me to conform, because she herself didn't conform, and however I might interpret this as an adult, to my young mind it sometimes seemed wrong. She didn't match my idea of a real mother, a typical mother, a good mother.

So who or what is a good mother? I can still remember, very clearly, one of my first maternity nurse postings. I went to work for Sara, a north London mother who had just had her second baby. It was a six-week booking and Sara wanted help getting the baby into a routine while she also coped with looking after her three-year-old, Thomas. Sara was an action woman, full of the kind of energy that made me feel exhausted just watching her. Her husband didn't earn much, but she was a high-powered banker and the main breadwinner at a time when that wasn't common. In fact, at that time a lot of women still expected to give up work when their babies came along. Sara truly believed she could have it all, and that belief gave her a lot of power; but she was also a sensitive woman who longed to be liked and accepted. That's why she was keen on attending the local mother and toddler group. She'd missed out when Thomas was a baby because she'd gone back to work when he was three months old. This time around, she was eager to get out and meet other mothers in the same situation.

Sara discovered a playgroup for the under-fives held at the local church hall, and insisted I went too. I suspect that she was nervous, despite her confident exterior, and wanted some moral support. I got the children ready while Sara agonised over what she should wear. Finally she settled on a smart skirt, high-heeled boots and a jacket. 'It's playgroup you're going to, not a business meeting,' I said, as she combed her hair and perfected her make-up. 'I want to make a good impression on the other mothers,' Sara explained, as she twirled in front of the mirror. She looked great, especially considering she'd had a baby only a few weeks before. So we all set off together, Sara and Thomas skipping in front while I pushed the baby in his pram.

This part of London wasn't smart and the church hall was run-down and grubby. Groups of mothers were hanging about, some holding babies, and in the middle of the floor a little army of toddlers dashed about or crawled on the dirty floor with some well-used toys. I'm very keen on cleanliness and I had to stop myself going in search of a mop! Almost as soon as we entered, I noticed the looks. The other mothers glanced over, looked Sara up and down, and turned away. She didn't seem to notice but took Thomas to the mess in the middle of the room and started showing him how to play with some of the toys. I could tell she wasn't making a great impression, even though no one had spoken to her. Then I heard one muttering, 'It's all right for some people who don't have to change nappies themselves.' Sara's smart clothing and neat appearance had gone down very badly. She looked out of place among the jeans and unkempt hair. When it came down to it, Sara didn't look like a mother. At least, she didn't look like the other mothers.

I didn't say anything to Sara about the frosty atmosphere at the playgroup – I assumed she'd noticed it herself – and was surprised when she was keen to go back the following week. She didn't get quite so dressed up this time, but she was still smart with neat hair. It was the same attitude again: she tried to break into a few groups and start conversation, but the other women were chilly. It was clear that they considered her selfish in some way for looking so well turned out: who has time to look like that, other than a pampered mother who puts herself first? There seemed to be an unspoken assumption that the more you neglect yourself, the better you must be as a mother, because you are selfless. Some of the women seemed to wear personal neglect with pride, as a 'good mother' badge. By extension, Sara must be a bad, selfish mother since she took time over herself. Not only that, but it probably looked as if she had a maternity nurse to do all the hard work. In actual fact, Sara was very hands-on and we shared it all.

By the time I left Sara after six weeks, she'd stopped going to the playgroup. I saw that the hostility there was getting her down. But she was a fighter and refused to let it defeat her. Instead, she met up with old friends and told me that she'd be going back to work when the baby was six months old. I've never forgotten that early experience. I hadn't seen mothers interacting in this way and it had made me curious. I'd expected mothers always to be supportive of each other, but this wasn't Sara's experience. She hadn't conformed to their notions of what a good mother ought to be – and they punished her for it by excluding her. I have devoted a whole chapter to the subject of mothers at war with each other (see Chapter 5), my interest in which began with this experience early in my career.

Sara seemed like a good mother to me. She loved her children and she was determined to make their home a happy place and their lives healthy and well rounded. She just didn't intend to flog herself to death doing it, and in this Sara reminded me of my own mother. Yet despite an unconventional home life, I firmly believe my mother, too, was a good mother – even though she raised me contrary to the advice I offer mothers today. So how do we decide what makes a good mother? The question is complex and multi-layered, influenced by changing fashions in childcare and bound up in psychology. Nevertheless, we need to try and find an answer, for today we are more obsessed than ever about determining what a good mother is. More than that, our society is questioning whether or not we should have children at all. Becoming a parent is now a lifestyle choice and perhaps this is why there is so much pressure to get it right. After all, if you have chosen to sacrifice freedom, time and money on having children, then there is no room for failure.

It seems that we might define motherhood in a range of ways – as the creation of new life; or as a relationship – the bond between mother and child; or it might also be summarised as a series of tasks – making sure a child is fed and cared for; or we could define it as the responsibility of shaping and preparing a person to fit into society. In reality, it is a mish-mash of all these things, and it is how that mixture is made up that causes debate and disagreement. Mothering and the issues surrounding it strike to the core of ourselves, for the way we are raised affects who *we* are and, consequently, the way we raise our children affects who *they* are. The responsibility is formidable and this sense of overwhelming duty may be one reason why the debates on childcare are fierce and why some factions refuse to listen to others – and, boy, do I know about that. For every person who believes fervently in demand feeding and co-sleeping, there is another who believes just as intensely in the opposite. The chances are that both will raise normal, happy children – yet both will go on believing that only their way is the correct one.

Interestingly, when there is so much to unite parents, it is mothers themselves who often stand divided. Encouraged by the media, mothers put themselves into camps (breast versus bottle, sleep-training versus co-sleeping, career versus full-time parenting) and then pit themselves against one another. Mothers are generally in agreement on their broad hopes and ambitions for their child, so why do they allow themselves to get into battle over methods? One of the answers lies in the negative experiences many have had, which make them feel under attack for choices they have made. Ironically, it seems to me it's the overwhelming range of choices available that often lies at the root of the problem. When I first started my career mothers had far less choice. Baby clothing and equipment would be passed from family to family, and traditional methods of education and discipline were adopted with little thought given to alternative approaches. Nowadays there is an endless choice of baby equipment and products, and information overload on every aspect of a child's welfare and development. Too much choice can be oppressive rather than liberating; mothers can become obsessed with trying to make the perfect choices and end up stricken with anxiety when they think they've got it wrong. The very fact that people do things in so many different ways muddies the waters when it comes to our efforts to determine what a good mother is.

I've cared for over 300 babies in the course of my career, and I've met a great many more mothers from all over the world, from different cultures and social backgrounds. British nannies are frequently in demand abroad as they are often appointed to change the traditional methods of upbringing in a culture: for example, children who are carried for much of the time, spoon-fed until they are five years old and who co-sleep with parents. The traditional methods are not wrong, but younger generations often feel they have to make changes in order that their children can cope better in modern society. I have been incredibly lucky and privileged to have had such a rich and varied career. I have worked with ordinary, hard-working parents of twins in a one-bedroom flat in north London, and at the other extreme was once employed by royalty in the Middle East, where I lived in a pink palace with only one young child to look after, my own bodyguards and a football team of servants. I have worked with a family in Manchester who were struggling with health and financial worries, followed by a wealthy Chinese family who lived in a stunning house in the most exclusive area of Hong Kong. I've gone from chateaux in Switzerland to the bush in South Africa, where families with eight children had to live in one room. Yet for every difference I observed between these diverse groups, there were also a great many similarities. The one thing I am aware of is that 'All mothers are different'. Like the babies they give birth to, they come in all shapes, sizes and personalities.

Across the globe, each mother has her own unique set of circumstances to cope with as she faces the enormous challenge of raising a child. One might have a big house and all the latest baby equipment, but her husband won't so much as hold the baby while she takes a shower; another might live on a shoestring but have the most wonderfully supportive family and friends. I know of women who fantasised about the perfect baby and idyllic family life, only to be shocked and depressed by the reality of a crying infant and the exhaustion that goes with caring for it. Others, sometimes the most unlikely, have had very easy babies and take to motherhood with breezy carelessness. Some mothers are eaten up with anxiety about doing the right thing, yet others have never given a thought to what they do, or why they do it. I've worked with mothers of babies who have screamed remorselessly from day one, and sick babies who have never slept more than two hours at a time. I've also known mothers of bouncing, ravenous, blooming children. Through this complex maze of circumstance and personality can there possibly be a single route to good motherhood?

It is impossible to create a set of rules that will work perfectly for every family: even if it were possible, it would not guarantee a problem-free child. Yet Western society seems set on finding that one recipe. Imagine a woman who has always been able to control her environment and who perhaps has never held an infant until the arrival of her first baby. Then take away the traditional support networks – her extended family and other mothers in the community – and leave her to cope alone. Next, bombard her with scientific research about this and that, have one medical expert tell her authoritatively what she must do for the good of the child and another tell her the opposite, then frighten her with disastrous consequences if she fails to do the right thing. Give her magazines that will depress the hell out of her with images of celebrity mums back in their size 8 jeans a week after they've given birth. Finally, fill her television screen and newspapers with righteous attacks on mothers as the cause of all society's ills, from antisocial behaviour in teenagers to rising levels of obesity. Is it any wonder that she is anxious? Is it surprising that she feels constantly judged and sure to fail?

Parenting is one of the subjects on which strangers feel at liberty to offer an opinion. Faye, a new mother, told a colleague of mine that she was feeding her baby a bottle of expressed milk in a park when a woman she'd never met before rebuked her for not breast-feeding her child. 'And the worst thing was,' she told my colleague, 'I didn't tell this woman that it was none of her business how I fed my child. I got all flustered and explained that actually I did breast-feed my child, and that this was expressed breast milk and not formula. But I don't understand why I felt I had to justify myself.'

Faye's reaction is understandable. Society's image of the good mother is of the mother devoted to her child, who puts the needs of that child above her own. The mother who works has to excuse herself, the woman who doesn't breast-feed has to explain herself and the woman who puts her children into routines must hide her secret lest people think she is a cruel mother who heartlessly leaves her baby to cry. Believe me, I know the vicious and unfair criticism the follower of routines can receive. The fact is, individuals feel able to criticise mothers and interfere in the way they bring up their children, and do so in a manner they would never dream of adopting elsewhere. The effect of such criticism is eroded confidence and increased guilt as women grapple to get to grips with motherhood.

Early in my career, my phone rang in the middle of the night. This is not an unusual occurrence – the early hours of the morning are when I get calls from women whose fears have come to torment them. I knew the mother on the other end of the line. She was strong and healthy, in a happy relationship and financially secure. Her home in Fulham, west London, was comfortable and beautifully furnished. She was a woman who seemed to have it all. Now here she was, sobbing down the telephone. 'I feel so frightened and alone, as though I'm in the middle of a desert,' she said. 'I've got my baby here with me. He's fine, yet I feel as though I'm in hell and can't cope. I'm terrified and I don't know who I am any more, but there's absolutely no one to turn to.' Her voice has haunted me ever since and it changed my perspective on life. I think so often about how lonely and frightened she felt. At the time, all I could do was listen and reassure her that many other mothers had the same feelings. Many times women have told me that they sit nursing their babies in the middle of the night, consumed with fear of doing something wrong, fear of being alone and fear that they no longer recognise who they are. Sometimes I wake up in the middle of the night and I wonder how many women are out there feeling desperate. Many women seem to have it all, but in spite of this, huge numbers feel vulnerable and lonely.

Cassie (40) told me:

I became a mother at the age of 36, which was possibly a little late. You don't have the same energy then as you did in your twenties.

We moved to a new town a long way from family and friends when Eliza was born and I was lonely and isolated. I didn't have a postnatal support group of friends and my husband's absences meant I did everything alone. If there had been more money I would have loved to get some domestic help. There have been times I have felt desperate for help. I had a straightforward, natural birth but I felt that labour was a sort of death. I felt as if I was dying. Yet I was in hospital for just one day and both Eliza and I were well, and recovered quickly. The reality of motherhood can be utterly bewildering. To care for a child, alone, creates huge mental pressures.

When Eliza was a baby, I felt blissed-out by the experience. I submerged myself utterly in her babyhood and I felt tremendously happy to have a purpose. My husband worked away from home a lot and Eliza and I existed in a little bubble of our own. It was only when she was about two that I realised how much independence I had lost. It crept up on me gradually as the exhaustion kicked in. She never slept well and I had no sort of routine. It hit me then just how hard being a mother was.

Culturally, women are sexual beings until they become mothers. Invisibility sets in then and I found the shock intense. There are celebrity mums out there who appear to have it all. Women like Madonna and Cherie Blair, who has four kids and is a barrister, are held up as wonder women. But there is no cultural myth to reflect the transition, or the phases of change from sex bomb to mother. I looked for icons of feminism to help me find the way through and I found none outside the pages of glossy magazines. The loss of freedom and mental space leaves you floundering. I was gripped by a ferocious love for my daughter, but had little idea of how to fit myself into the picture. Becoming a mother is like entering unfamiliar territory without any map or signpost. You are left to stumble over the terrain without guidance or preparation.

If motherhood was a shock for Cassie, for others it's an easy transition. The quiet time in the middle of the night when they are feeding their babies is, for them, the best part of the day. It is a magical time when they can enjoy the stillness and appreciate the miracle of new life. But does the peaceful pleasure, or the ease of the transition to motherhood, experienced by one make her a better mother than the woman who is sitting depressed and anxious? Over the years many people have said to me, 'You must love babies very much to have worked with them for so many years', but I have also loved working with the mums, who have taught me so much. I have often been involved in stressful situations where many tears have been shed, but have also experienced a lot of love and laughter. One of the most satisfying aspects of my career has been the opportunity to make this very precious time with a new baby a happy time for all the family.

Turning to history, would the fear and anxiety women face be less of an issue if the burden on mothers hadn't increased over recent generations? Until the development of psycho-analysis in the 1890s, little thought was given to the notion of what made a good mother. Children were God-given, their characters part of their essential nature. Less well off mothers were unable to spare the time to worry about what effect they were having on their children; in the middle and upper classes, young babies were often sent away to be wet-nursed and brought up during their infancy by village women, who raised them as their own. The idea that the mother had a role that no one else could fill did not exist. It wasn't until the nineteenth century that the concept of 'good' parenthood emerged, and focus moved to the mother and her skills. As the middle classes grew stronger and more powerful as the dominant group in British society, they hired help in the home, but tended to play a bigger role in parenting than the social classes above and below them did.

In the early 1900s infant mortality, caused by poor living conditions and appalling standards of health, was so high that the state intervened in childcare to prevent what was called 'national suicide'. Then, once mothering techniques began to be explored, three important things happened. The first was that the concept of a 'good mother', as opposed to a 'bad mother', became widespread (and you could only be one or the other). The second was the growth of opposing schools of thought, which added to the general confusion about what the right methods should be. Thirdly, the burden of responsibility began to fall on one woman alone – the mother.

Childcare theories before the Second World War were strict and rigid, but post-war ideas became more child-centred and permissive, until ultimately they focused entirely on the needs of the child and not at all on the needs of the mother. At the same time, a mythical view emerged of motherhood as home-based, child-centred and completely fulfilling emotionally. It became embedded in Western consciousness that a woman's place was in the home, that her life found its meaning in raising children and that if she did this correctly and was a 'good mother' she would need nothing else. These theories put the onus of childcare firmly on the mother. During the war, women had challenging jobs, but when the war was over and men returned wanting their jobs back, women had little choice but to retreat to the home. The image of the flawless fifties housewife and mother, eager to produce the perfect home and children, was formed.

This stereotype was so powerful that we are still wrestling with it today. It is a false one, of course. For one thing, even in the 1950s most housewives had domestic help of some kind, or at least family nearby. Mothers were rarely left alone to cope and they didn't experience the kind of eerie loneliness that modern mothers can suffer when they suddenly find them-selves at home all day with a new baby to care for. The guilt and confusion that women feel as they experience mother-hood have increased immeasurably over the last fifty years. At the same time as struggling to win equality in the workplace, women feel undermined by society's assumption that they ought to devote themselves entirely to their children. As women's liberation movements grew in the 1960s and 1970s, feminism found itself in a dilemma. Women still wanted to have families, and they knew that children could bring them happiness and fulfilment, but they also wanted social and financial equality and to compete in a man's world. Today's women may feel simultaneously liberated and shackled as a result of these frequently conflicting objectives, and forty years on there are still no universal solutions.

During the early years of my growing up my mother and I reversed roles many times. Sometimes she was the mother and I was the daughter; then later when she was suffering the debilitating illness of rheumatoid arthritis and deep vein thrombosis I became the mother and she became the daughter. Whichever one of us adopted the role of mother was always caring, understanding and supportive of the other. But during those years there were also times when neither of us was the mother or daughter and we became more like sisters. Laughing and loving each other at times; fighting like cat and dog at other times.

I recall a time when we must have been going through a stage of me being Mummy and Mummy being me – or perhaps even more like conspiring sisters. We had decided that a new carpet was needed for the sitting room. After several days of drafting a letter to our local furniture shop my mother sent me into town to choose the carpet. Pride of place in the room was given to the Queen Anne antique sideboard. Okay it was a replica, but boy was she proud of it. The rest of the room was in keeping with the embossed floral wallpaper and sideboard: deep red 100 per cent cotton velvet curtains, and a red and cream embossed three-piece suite that we were only ever allowed to sit on when people came to visit.

I will never quite know what she was thinking that day when she sent me into town to choose the carpet. But I entered the furniture shop feeling very important and confident. After several hours of browsing through umpteen carpet sample books I made my decision. I felt so proud that I had chosen the carpet of my mother's dreams and was sure that she would be proud of me too. That evening she repeatedly asked me; what is it like, what is it like? Taking the mother's role, I was firm. At the wise old age of 12 I reassured her that it would be the best surprise of her life – she would love it.

Eight days later the big moment arrived. I insisted that my mother go and have coffee with a neighbour until the new carpet was fully fitted and all the furniture was back in its former place. Then, and only then, could she view her precious sitting room in its new splendour. I will never forget the moment when she entered the room. It was equivalent to Laurence Llewelyn-Bowen and Linda Barker's worst nightmare. As a child I could only see the most fantastic carpet, vibrant in every psychedelic colour you could imagine. Purple and orange swirls were intertwined with green and brown circles. She took one look and yelled for Granda: 'Dad, I'm taking one of my dizzy turns.' It took at least a week for her to recover from the shock.

Now, as you read this you are probably thinking: well, stupid woman, what did she expect, sending a kid to choose a carpet? If we are going to fit mothers into rigid good mother and bad mother categories she would probably fit in the category of bad mother for putting the responsibility on me at such a young age. But she was far from being a bad mother: inexperienced, lacking in knowledge, yes – but certainly not a bad mother.

And does being a good mother matter? I often ask myself this when I see women blaming and punishing themselves – and each other – for not being perfect. It might seem a strange question, for of course it matters in principle: good mothers bring up good and happy children, and society needs good people. That sounds simple enough, but I know warm and wonderful people whose childhoods were not exactly model. Equally, an idyllic childhood does not always produce a happy and well-balanced individual. When I meet new people, I cannot guess what their upbringings were like. If I learn more about their background, I might see how certain aspects of their personalities make sense in the context of their life experience, but I could never say, 'Jane was brought up like this, because she acts like that.' If it were that simple, the whole nature/nurture argument would be at an end. Indeed, sometimes the opposite of what is expected can be true: women who try desperately to be good mothers can spoil and smother their children, while mothers who are apparently indifferent can produce independent children who are a pleasure to be around. So why do we need to know what a good mother is, and why should mothers aspire to be one? What difference will it make?

Sally (29) told me:

I always knew I wanted to be 'a good mother'. I felt it was more important than being good at my job or a good friend or daughter. A good mother must be a good person; a bad mother must be a bad person. It's that simple. I had a very happy childhood and I think that's why I feel so deeply that I want the same thing for my son. My mother worked while she was bringing us up, but as she was an illustrator of children's books, her job didn't take her out of the home much and I remember her being around for most of my childhood. We lived in a small town and when she wasn't there, the key was under the doormat and there was a cake in the tin. I never felt neglected, even when she wasn't at home. She was more eccentric than most of the mothers I knew, and I think that has given me confidence, but mostly I remember her being there and always feeling secure, supported and loved.

Sally's mother broke the mould of her own childhood. Her own mother was a wealthy woman who believed completely in nannies and restricted parental care. Sally's mother consulted her old nanny for advice on how to bring up her children, and balanced her work outside the home with her desire to raise her children in a more hands-on way than she herself had experienced. Sally herself had a career in the civil service, but she gave it up to be a full-time mother to her son. To her, good mothering means being the major shaping force in a child's life for as long as possible. If Sally is the result of a 'good mother' – a stable, happy person able to analyse and pass on the effects – then she is a rare example indeed. Many people can point to unhappiness in their early life, or have feelings of anger or resentment about the way they were brought up. Modern psychology teaches us to search in our past for explanations and causes of our present unhappiness and shortcomings. This can liberate us from the burden of our own failure, but it also imposes upon us a monumental burden of responsibility for someone else's success – our children's.

Eileen (46) is the eldest of five children and was brought up in Glasgow:

I was born out of wedlock at a time when society still frowned upon unmarried mothers. My mother felt under pressure to marry and did so when I was one year old, but not to my father, who had long since deserted her. I don't think my mother was in love with my stepfather, and although they have grown closer over the years, she has always resented me for causing the dissatisfaction and unhappiness in her life. I think there was something about me that reminded her of my father's rejection and, as a result, I never felt loved or wanted. My mother adored my three younger brothers and my sister, the baby of the family, but I was always the odd one out and never felt as though I belonged. I always got the blame for everything and was frequently beaten or sent to bed early. In fact, looking back, I think I spent most of my childhood in my bedroom. I always had a difficult relationship with my mother and as a teenager I was so unhappy that I couldn't wait to leave home. When I was 16, I met a man who was ten years older than me. I jumped at the chance of marriage, mainly to escape my mother, but it was a loveless marriage and, on top of that, he drank excessively and often hit me after his many drinking sessions. I endured nearly 20 years of misery before I eventually found enough courage to leave him. Yet, despite everything, I have produced two of the most wonderful children. My son has a good job with the police and my daughter is currently at university. I consciously brought them up in a way that was completely different to my upbringing and I have always been very close to both of them. I was strict, but I never hit them and was always as open, honest and loving as I could be. We are in touch with each other almost every day and they share everything with me, both good and bad. I still have a very strained relationship with my own mother, but despite everything, thanks to the warm relationship I have with my children, I consider myself lucky.

Eileen's background could not have been more different from Sally's, yet both have turned out to be warm and sympathetic individuals and good mothers. Sally put into words what is deeply embedded in society's subconscious – that a good woman will be a good mother, and vice versa. Further, we believe that a good mother will know instinctively how to be one. Jean Liedloff's book *The Continuum Concept*, an influential work of the 1970s, advocates a 'return' to an intense form of childcare where the baby is constantly held. Liedloff, a psychotherapist who studied the tribes of South America, was the founder of the still popular theory of attachment parenting. She said, 'I would be ashamed to admit to the Indians that where I come from the women do not feel themselves capable of raising children until they read the instructions written by a strange man.' In one sentence, Liedloff implied a great many things. In particular, that the Indians, through allowing their instinct to guide their approach to mothering, are good and natural, while Western women fail by not trusting their instinct and are, therefore, bad and unnatural mothers.

Lori (39), a dance instructor, was not unusual in telling me how much this idea of 'instinct' had bewildered and worried her.

During my pregnancy, I assumed that instinct was completely natural and when the baby arrived I would somehow know what to do. I thought that looking at my baby would kick-start my 'instinct' and all would be clear. I just went from one antenatal check-up to the next and didn't look beyond the birth. I believed that instinct was completely natural. I had no idea how to look after a child. I believed others when they told me that everything would come naturally. In fact, it was a terrible shock to find myself without a clue what to do with this tiny baby! I didn't know why she was crying and no matter how hard I tried to 'tune in' to her needs, I was completely in the dark. I felt like a failure for the first few months because I believed that this vital thing mothers had – instinct – was missing in me.

Wendy (33) said:

You know you're meant to listen to your instinct, but there are all these other opinions coming at you from every direction. There are the books you read, the television and newspapers, not to mention the midwife, the antenatal teacher and the health visitor. Add in your mother, your mother-in-law, all your friends and the old lady on the bus and it's pretty much impossible to trust your instinct. I was so terrified that my baby was going to die, that my instincts were all over the place.

My own view is that modern mothers are being horribly let down by a system that pushes them out of hospital (sometimes only hours after the birth of their child) and sends them home with their tiny bundle, only to be told to trust their instinct.

Paula (43) recently had her first baby. She told me:

> I'm used to being in charge of things and, as an older mother, I somehow felt that my life experience would help me care for a new baby. I don't know why I should have thought that, but I did. I'd had a natural birth with only minimal intervention, so I was discharged about 18 hours after the birth. I hated being in hospital – the noise, the discomfort, the loneliness and the fear of germs. I desperately wanted to be in my own home, so when they said I could go I didn't hesitate. With hindsight, I should have stayed as long as possible. Once home, I felt under pressure to be up and about too soon. I hadn't established breastfeeding, had awful problems and the support network just wasn't there. The midwives were supposed to come every day for the first ten days, but I only saw a midwife on the second day and then two others a week apart after that. As for the six-week check-up, I didn't realise it was supposed to be my health check. I thought it was about the baby, so the doctor didn't even look me over. I feel horrified now at how alone I was. Thank God my husband is extremely supportive and somehow we managed to get through it.

The modern preoccupation with women being strong and capable means that many of them are afraid to admit to weakness or to needing help. They assume that everyone else has got it right and they are the only ones feeling frightened and vulnerable. This is particularly true of new mothers, who generally deserve far more support than they are getting. In my experience in many different cultures – including Arab,

Indian and Jew – there is a much greater sense of family and the arrival of a baby is a joyous event to be shared and celebrated by everyone. New mothers are cosseted and are never left to cope alone. In a Chinese family in Hong Kong with whom I worked, following the birth of the baby, the mother was expected to enjoy a period of rest, when she was put on a special diet and looked after by family members. This extra support was an excellent thing for both mother and baby, and something that I have found sadly lacking in many Western societies. In less well-off communities, support is often still there in some form, and at the other extreme the wealthy can afford to pay for help, but there is a vast swathe of mothers in the middle who cannot afford support and whose extended families are scattered. These women usually have to cope very much alone, and they can feel pathetic and inadequate asking for help.

This insecurity is compounded by society's idea of what a good mother should look like. My mother was considered improper because of the way she took care of her appearance, but today the pendulum has swung in the opposite direction and there is pressure on mothers to be unrealistically glamorous. Celebrity mothers shed their pregnancy weight in the way only a wealthy woman can, helped by expert cooks and personal trainers and often already predisposed to be slender. This apparent ability to care for a new baby while still finding time to look slim and attractive may make other mothers feel inadequate and resentful, as in the earlier case of Sara (p.9). Recently I read about a celebrity mother-to-be who revealed that she had begun her post-pregnancy diet while still pregnant, on the basis that if she never gained the weight she'd never have to lose it.

What is a Good Mother?

When I compare mothering in my own childhood and the mothering taking place today, I can't help but think that this is not an easy time in history for women. I have spent my whole working life trying to help mothers. I have sat with women in their nighties at three in the morning and comforted them while they sobbed their hearts out from exhaustion and fear about their babies. When mothers ask me what I think the most important aspect of being a good mother is, many are surprised by my response. I think they expect me to pinpoint a certain part of the routines I encourage, or a certain view as to what makes a contented baby. However, I always say that what is most important is not just how long a baby sleeps, or who has been most successful in the baby routines, but also how happy and fulfilled a mother is. In my opinion, a happy and fulfilled mother is much more likely to meet her baby's needs and have a contented baby – regardless of whether a mother follows routines or takes the attachment parenting approach. Finding what is right for you is the key.

Some fortunate mothers find complete fulfilment in their baby. However, if this leads to the exclusion of their husband or partner it is not always a healthy long-term happiness. Most mothers I have worked with do find their babies enormously rewarding and engaging, but still wish to have another dimension to their lives. And some of the mothers I have helped find motherhood both stressful and unfulfilling. It is for all these mothers that I have been encouraged to write this book.

I am sure some people will ask how I can have the nerve to write a book about a subject when I have never had the pleasure of 'front-line' experience. It is a cause of sadness to me that I never had a family of my own; however, I do not feel that this hinders me in my wish to help mothers everywhere when they ask for help. In fact, perhaps by never having my own children, I have been able to retain a healthy detachment when witnessing the rollercoaster experience of new motherhood.

Some of the mothers I have worked with are themselves role models to the next generation of women. During the last 20 years, the pattern of women's lives has changed enormously. In the early days of my work as a maternity nurse, the very high-powered career women I helped were the exception not the norm. They were in uncharted waters, breaking glass ceilings and redefining family life. The husbands were either their career equal or perhaps their support. These days it is unusual for me to find myself helping a woman who has not had some sort of career. Often it is the career and the draw of the other life which motivates them to organise help before the birth and ensure that early motherhood is, as far as possible, a stress-free and manageable experience.

Young women in their early twenties today expect both to be mothers and have careers. This is indeed a balance that requires some careful management. Like the babies they give birth to, the one thing that all new mothers have in common is that they require their basic needs to be met. Like their babies, they need to be loved and nurtured. Babies who are fed well, loved much and have all their basic needs met will grow into happy and content human beings. The same goes for mothers. Sometimes my advice to them seems pretty flippant: shave your legs and paint your toenails, I tell them. And I mean it! Feel good about yourself. Take care of yourself. Ask for help. Tell the truth about how you feel to your friends. Don't, please, kill yourself trying to be perfect.

All my skills and knowledge have been learned from my own mother, from the other mother figures in my life, from mothers who have written books and from the thousands of mothers I have talked to over the last two decades. I am so grateful for everything they have taught me.

Of all the mothers who have asked me, 'Am I a good mother?' I can assure you that you are almost certainly a good mother. Because you wouldn't ask that question if you weren't.

❀

Chapter 2

My Mother, My Best Friend

❀

Although I was not born in Edinburgh I fell in love with the city when I first left home at 16 and attended college there. It is the place where I met the man who became the love of my life, my soul mate and my best friend for ten years. We met when I was 16 and he was 18. They say that you never forget your first love and I think this is very true. There is something so special, so sweet and so innocent about a first love, especially when you are as young as we were. We thought that together we could conquer the world, and for ten years we travelled it together, grew up together and sadly during that growing up period we also grew apart.

I was 26 when I flew back to Edinburgh, broken-hearted that I had lost the love of my life. It was during those early months after the break-up of my marriage that my relationship with my mother took another twist. In the years that followed we continued to reverse the roles of our mother–daughter relationship, but we also formed another relationship. We became best friends.

It was on a very cold night in November that this friendship with my mother was formed, a friendship that was to last for the rest of her life, one that was filled with more love and laughter than anyone could ever wish for.

I had arrived back from South Africa emotionally, mentally and financially broken. On that November night my mother and I sat up in my bed, huddled together making plans for how I was to survive and rebuild my life. Life looked so bleak that night. The electricity had been cut off because I could not pay the bill; I had spent my last couple of pounds on a fish supper. But my mother still managed to see the funny side of things as she divided the fish supper up between the two of us and 'my babies'. Tammy Toots, Mrs Pussy and George, my three cats, were made to sit in a straight row at the bottom of the bed alongside Henry the dog.

She would roar with laughter each time she threw a chip in the air to see which one them would catch it first. Despite shedding bucketloads of tears, I could not help but laugh at the same time. It's your best friend who knows how to make you laugh when times are tough.

During the months that followed we conspired, just as we had when I was a child about how to get the baker to leave us some free cream buns. A plan of action was cooked up, such as only two best friends could invent. The first thing my mother advised was that I had to get out and about and meet other young people. But as I had not lived in Edinburgh for ten years I had lost touch a long time ago with any friends I had made from college.

During the months she stayed with me my mother took a job as a night carer to help me get back on track financially. I recall when she got that first pay packet. True to my mother's unique way of thinking, she did not pay the electric bill: instead she went out and bought me a pair of black velvet pedal-pushers and a very sexy cream silk blouse. She said, 'Gina, we must get our priorities right, and right now you need to get out and about, so we don't bloody need any electricity – you can have a bath at Mrs-B-up-the-doors's every night, and when it gets dark we have the candles.' Next on her list of priorities was the following advert she placed in the *Scotsman*:

Young, slim, attractive, well-travelled female seeks to meet young, handsome, sensual, fun-loving, non-smoking, intelligent male with GSOH for fun times.

My God – did the fun times begin!

I received nearly 150 replies, mainly from middle-class professional men from the world of business, banking and law. My mother and I spent hours poring over all the letters, giggling like teenagers as we put letters and photographs into categories – most handsome, most intelligent, etc.

Looking back now, it seems ridiculous that two women, one aged 26 and the other 46, had not a clue how to approach dating. Years later when we used to recall that period of my life my mother would say, 'Gina, there was an excuse for you, you were young, but what on earth was my excuse? I was your mother – I should have had more sense.'

Well, I suppose it was an unusual way to break into the dating circuit. In the months that followed I dated more men than most girls probably date in a lifetime. I met every single guy that responded. My mother went along on nearly every date, and the pair of us would giggle our way throughout the evening as we vetted them. I imagine now that some of these guys must have been shocked at the audacity of my mother and me, as we were downright blunt when we made comments or questioned their appearance or their shoes.

While I was intelligent and travelled, university-educated I was not, and as much as I love Edinburgh some of the people here are obsessed with which school or university they attended. I can now imagine how strange they thought the pair of us, as my mother would tell them: 'I never went to school much, and never bothered sending Gina if she didn't want to go.'

However, I must have done something right on those dates because in the months that followed there was not a lunch or dinner when I did not meet up with either a highly charged businessman, an ambitious young banker or an up-and-coming lawyer. Having only ever been out with one guy in my life, it was like taking a crash course on understanding men. I found that doctors were the ones that drank the most, accountants and bankers definitely spent less money on dates, and lawyers would always try to get you into bed on the first date.

Like two 17-year-olds, my mother and I would discuss each date at great length and how best to proceed with a particular guy. Given that her experience with men was even more limited than mine, it is not surprising that I never got into a serious relationship with any of these men. Her view was much the same as when I was 16 – that all men would want sex and that was normal, but nice girls did not do it until after they were married.

I think these guys must have thought I was nuts when I

giggled and said sorry I don't kiss or hold hands until the third date! I have to say that while it was an old-fashioned approach, it certainly kept the men keen. I had some fantastic, funny times and made great friends of some of these guys. But the one thing that I did realise is that they were looking for a serious relationship, and of course I was having far too much fun having so many guys wooing me that I certainly was not going to settle for the attention of just one man.

During that frenetic dating time of my life I learned a lot about my mother as a woman and our exploits around the bars, restaurants and cafés in Edinburgh helped bond our best friend relationship. The other great thing about having your mother as your best friend is that there is not the competitiveness that can arise between two women of the same age who are best friends – and your mother certainly does not try to steal your boyfriends!

While we would often have a minor fall-out there was only ever one major row during that period, and like everything that happened between my mum and myself, it was extreme. It happened one Saturday night when a doctor I was dating had to cancel as he had been called to the hospital on an emergency. By 9pm I was pacing the floor frantic to go out and have some fun. I begged and pleaded with my mum to come with me to the disco in the Royal Mile. She was adamant that she would not. 'I don't mind going to the pub or a nice cocktail bar with you but I draw the line at a disco.' I cried, begged and stamped my feet like I did when I was eight years old, but instead of yelling, 'I want a real mummy', I shouted, 'Some best friend you've turned out to be – I want a real best friend.'

She relented and by 10pm we were legging our way up the

Royal Mile to the disco. It did not for one moment dawn on me that she might feel uncomfortable or look out of place in a disco where the average age was 20 to 30. I pushed her through the crowds at the bar and got her seated in a fairly quiet corner with a brandy and ginger ale, which was her favourite drink. The song 'I will survive' was belting out and the dance floor was heaving. Forget Gina Ford 'The Queen of Routines': in those days it was Queen of the Dance Floor, and once I got on to it it would be hours before I got off.

It was no different that night. I danced and sang for hours before I even gave my mother a thought. When I eventually made my way back to the corner where she was sitting I was faced with an image that has stayed strong in my mind for many years. My mother's normally smiley happy face and twinkling eyes looked like thunder. Her hands were clenched tightly around the handle of the brolly that matched her tweed Burberry suit, that matched the silk headscarf that was still tightly tied around her chin. While we did laugh later about the incident and how hilarious and out of place she had looked in the disco, she said to me that night: 'Honey, I am your mother and your best friend, and there is virtually nothing that I wouldn't do for you – but never, ever ask me to go to a disco with you again.'

As the months went by I did start to make other young friends to go out with in Edinburgh and my mother returned home to the husband she had abandoned for several months, safe in the knowledge that her 'pride and joy' was rebuilding her life.

I continued my dating and dancing frenzy for another year and made lots of fantastic female friends as well as men friends. But not one of them could ever hold a candle to the friendship that my mother and I formed during those months, and that continued for the rest of her life.

How different would things have been between us if I had been a boy? I sometimes wondered. Ask any mother of boys and you will be hard pushed to find one who will not confess to even a fleeting look of longing down the aisle of pink and lilac dresses. Mothers of sons often bemoan the dirty football boots and boisterous games. At the same time, many of these mothers have shared with me a secret relief that some of the more painful aspects of girlhood will be passing them by. Teenage girls can be bitchy to each other – and to their mothers. Somehow boys seem more straightforward, smelly socks aside.

But no mother of a boy expects to find a best friend figure in her son, although such relationships can develop. Somehow friendship is a special element of the relationship between a mother and a daughter. The mothers of young daughters who spoke to me explained that with a daughter a secret hope arrives: a possibility of closeness and intimacy for the rest of their lives together. Whether mums have been close to their own mothers or not, most seem to want to share things with their daughters. Trips to the hairdresser or beauty parlour, to manicurists and spas, or simply down to the shops, are the treasured realm of this closeness.

Janey (38) is the mother of three boys and she told me:

I wanted a daughter each time one of my boys was born. I wanted the intimacy of that relationship, the girliness, I suppose. My sons are pretty wild and I sometimes think a girl in the family would alter the dynamic. I might feel less outnumbered too! Even the dog is male. I think you also want a daughter who can take care of you when you are older. You expect to lose your sons to their own families one day – that old saying must have some truth.

We will see in later chapters how much the relationship between a mother and daughter can change when babies arrive on the scene. For some women it is a time of increased closeness with their mothers, a time when they turn to them for support and advice.

Sallie (31) writes:

My mother is my best friend and has been a tremendous support since the birth of my daughter. Prior to Maya's arrival Mum was always a first source of advice and she has always been there for me during any difficult periods in my life. When Maya was born she really looked after me in the first few months while I looked after the baby.

Our parenting styles are perhaps a little bit different in that I wasn't a 'routine' baby but more had to fit in with what was happening at the time (especially being a second child). I think Mum has been amazed by the amount of effort I have put into motherhood. We haven't as yet really disagreed on anything.

My relationship with my mother-in-law has perhaps improved since Maya's arrival as we have more in common now. Previously there had always been a sense of com-petition. Again I think I am a more focused and organised mother than she was and also perhaps a bit gentler – she

tends to get anxious when Maya cries. I feel that she sees
me as an equal now I am a mother.

Often what becomes an issue between a new mother and new
grandmother relates to child-rearing techniques and attitudes.
The generation gap throws up huge differences. The routines I
outline in my childcare books are contrary to the established
pattern in hospitals a generation or two ago. Many of today's
grandmothers would have stayed in hospital for up to two weeks.
Their babies were brought to them four-hourly for feeding and
then taken back to the nursery. The frequent result was that the
mother's milk would dry up long before she left the hospital.
During my work as a maternity nurse I realised that mothers
who wanted to breast-feed needed to establish a pattern of
feeding little and often in the early days. The rest is history, but I
often hear stories of mums who are choosing to follow my
routines and who encounter disapproval or downright horror
from their own mothers. This is hardly surprising considering
what information and guidance was available in their day
compared to now. And my book is only one of thousands,
packed full of advice for the modern mother. As discussed above,
weaning advice is now totally different from the way many
modern mums were weaned. How many conscientious mothers
of today have been appalled that Granny thinks the baby can
have a full Sunday lunch at three months? One mother told me
she had read that talcum powder contained carcinogens and
exploded in rage at her own mother when she found her liberally
slapping the talc on her precious baby. The poor grandmother
wasn't aware of science's latest pronouncements.

It's more than parenting techniques that a new generation

questions, however. The whole shebang comes under scrutiny as the new mother looks at her own childhood and makes changes to the things she found unhelpful while embracing positive and successful aspects of her mother's approach.

Camilla (32) writes:

My relationship with my mother is very strong. I wouldn't say she was my 'best friend' but she's certainly a rock in my life. I don't have the sort of relationship with my mum where I tell her everything – mostly because I don't want to be criticised! My sister has that kind of relationship with her, but I don't, I'm a much more closed book. I will speak to her about most things, just not everything. However, she has taught me about responsibility, and shown me endless loyalty, patience and unequivocal love during times when she could have – and maybe should have – given up. That is something I can never forget and will certainly carry through with Lola and any other children we may have.

I do try to do more with Lola than my mum did with me. I always remember school holidays being so boring. She'd promise to take me to butterfly houses or places like that, and never ever did. I could never understand the action of saying one thing or promising something and never delivering. She also can't swim or ride a bike, so I don't ever remember doing anything like that either. My father taught me how to ride a bike and how to swim, and we only had a family holiday twice. So the one thing I'll do differently is spend more quality time just doing 'stuff'.

This aside, my childhood was actually idyllic and I was without doubt very lucky and much loved by my mother.

Our parenting styles seem to differ in many ways, but I was a child of the seventies, and mum was (and still is) very conservative in her ways. Take controlled crying, for instance – something that my mother simply did not and would not do, and she also doesn't believe in routines: her stance is that all babies are different and they'll settle themselves in time. I think it took me about 20 years to settle myself! However, we agree on a lot of things and her support with doing things with Lola my way has been solid.

There are some unhappy stories too. Sometimes women with new babies feel their mothers are leaving behind their mothering role in their daughters' lives to take their rightful place at the top of the family ladder.

Grandparents today can enjoy a very different relationship with their grandchildren than they had themselves. Jan Hunt, writing about 'Empathetic Grandparenting', comments that, 'Fifty years ago, a grandchild was expected to show outward respect and courtesy to a grandparent with little regard to the way the grandparent treated the child, and with little regard for the child's true feelings.' She considers this both good and bad news for a grandparent who can no longer expect to be accorded traditional respect, but who can develop a genuine relationship that isn't based on a show of manners and a child's fear of punishment.

Grandmotherhood can be an extremely rewarding period of a woman's life. One third of grandmothers spend an equivalent of three days a week caring for their grandchildren. But when a grandmother stops being a mother, with all the best friend status she may have held in her daughter's life, it can cause a daughter a great deal of pain and feelings of abandonment.

Petra (29) told me:

Before I had my two children my relationship with my mother was a loving, caring one. My parents are very affectionate and loving. I had a very happy childhood. Mum was always there when I needed her, and vice versa. She really was my best friend and we told each other everything. I trusted her in every way. But no matter how well we got on, our views on children were always very different. I had watched, as a young adult, her spoiling my two younger nieces to a point where they had very little respect for her or appreciation for what was given to them. I always knew that if I ever had children I would have to be very firm with my mum so she wouldn't do the same with my children.

As I expected, our relationship very quickly changed once I had my first son. She adores children and she tended to take over. But as my approach to parenting was always going to be so much different to hers we had massive arguments and lots of tears were shed. I can't for one minute say I regret 'putting my foot down' but it saddens me deeply; I feel like the minute my son was born my mother stopped being my mother and is now *only* a grandmother. I know that if I were to ask her advice on something like tantrums she would always advise what she sees as best for my child – a short-term fix to stop him crying. She would bribe him and pander to his whims, whereas I have a more long-term view that this makes my and his life harder in the long run. So I had to very quickly decide boundaries and stick to them.

I feel I've lost my best friend now. Since I became a mother I actually need my mother to confide in and speak to more than ever, but her priority is always my children. I feel that I have served my purpose now by providing her with grandchildren. I always try to put my children's needs first, so it would be nice if I still had my mum to give me a hug on the not-so-good days. I wish that she could say, 'Hey, you are doing really well and have become a wonderful mum', but instead I always feel like she is disapproving of my methods.

When the relationship between a mother and daughter is altered by a new baby, there can be feelings of guilt and resentment on both sides. Very few mothers I spoke to have contradicted my view that a certain amount of respect is due to grandparents. The Old Testament commanded the Israelites to honour and esteem their elders, and in many cultures grandparents are held in the highest regard. I once worked for royalty in the Middle East where the grandmothers were treated like saints, and the grandchildren looked upon the grandmother as a second mother. What she said went. It was the same in the Chinese and Italian families I worked for: if the younger generation disagreed with the grandmother, they would never show it.

Even when the relationship between a mother and daughter is far from being that of best friends before a baby arrives, both parties seem to acknowledge that this is a time for change, for the balance within a family to adjust and for new boundaries to be drawn up.

Tara (36) writes:

I had a very difficult relationship with my mother as a teenager. I felt she didn't give me enough freedom and I rebelled against many of her constraints. My younger sister did not, thus making my normal teenage behaviour seem more extreme. Once I finished college and became financially independent things improved and I have enjoyed a close, loving relationship with her for the past 12 years, particularly since her own mother died. She is a very strong woman, who is very capable and practical and those are the qualities in her which I admire and have tried to emulate.

We do still have a parent/child relationship, however, and I feel she is judgemental about many of the things I believe and do, which were an issue when I was a teenager and have become so again since I became a mother. I don't always tell her the truth about the issues I have with Toby, since she is not an expert in my child. We have differences about feeding – I am keen for him not to be a fussy eater and so if he refuses what he is offered he doesn't get an alternative. My mother would certainly give him lots of sweets if she were allowed. I am a vegetarian and hoped to rear him as one also; this was very controversial with my mother and, because of concerns about weight gain, I have gone over to the dark side and am now giving him chicken.

We emigrated when Toby was nine months old, and I have felt immensely guilty about leaving my mother, although she has never made me feel that way. From the start of my pregnancy I have been very aware that he belongs to her too. I hope that my son grows up with the work ethic and good manners that my mother gave me, but I hope that he doesn't carry the fear of disappointing me.

One grandmother told me how astonished she was to discover that she loved her new grandchild as much as her own son, his father. That she could love someone who was not 100 per cent a blood relation took her by surprise and opened an unexpected reservoir of love in her, late in life. Of course, not everyone is able to access this and there are times when a relationship cannot be healed simply by the new bundle of joy.

Susie (32) writes:

> My relationship with my mother has never been great and it hasn't improved since I had my children. I had hoped that we might develop a grandmother/mother bond, but sadly not. She has always made it clear that she doesn't 'do' children. I feel sure that this is a front and I am sad that she is missing out on her grandchildren.
>
> Possibly this is because I left school at 16 and started working full-time. I quickly became very independent and have never really needed my mum since. Now I'm a mother I feel guilty about this, as I would hate my children not to need me.

For some women the lack of good mothering they themselves felt is an insurmountable problem, even when they reach motherhood. Yet they still use the mistakes they identify in their own childhood to try to improve the lot of the next generation. This is something I find extremely touching and which says a lot about the human spirit: that out of something unhappy and unsatisfactory there should be a determination for improvement.

Lyra (32):

Although my mother was in the background I was mainly raised by my nanny. I lived in Africa where it is common for the nanny to bath, feed and change nappies, to have sole care for children from early on. Before I had my own children I got on better with my mother than I do now. I feel strongly now that she was a 'lazy' parent – she participated in the easy elements of motherhood and the rest was left to the nanny. She didn't work, so really she had no excuse for being so hands-off. I do not parent like this. I do my best to research what is best for my children and I try to be as hands-on as possible when I'm around.

My parents were very accepting and had few boundaries. They had a lot of love for me, as did my nanny, so this was good. I think that my mother thought that having children would complete her. When we were not perfect this was difficult for her to accept and so until we were older we felt we always had to be 'good'. The words 'good' and 'naughty' are banned in my house.

The modern middle-class mother is often in her thirties or early forties. She has been independent of her own mother, perhaps for many years. Something I found over and over again in my research was how the distance of years between a mother and daughter could be covered in a short space of time once a baby is born. Many mothers feel excluded from their daughters' lives while the daughters are in their twenties. The middle-class, post-feminist woman tends to spend her twenties at college, travelling, getting a first job and generally enjoying a level of freedom and financial independence that can be a far cry from her own mother's experiences at that same age. A baby and the stable relationship and responsibility that mostly – but not always – come with that baby may close that gap in an astonishingly short time.

Serena (28) writes:

Before I had Maura my mother and I got on well – as long as we weren't living together. We saw each other occasionally at family gatherings. We were not very touchy-feely and were more like sisters. Since I had my baby, who is her first grandchild, she has completely changed. In the early days I felt totally lost and I relied heavily on my mother to help and guide me, as dealing with a newborn was totally new to me. She has been very respectful of the way I bring my baby up and only offers suggestions when I ask and has never pressured me to do anything her way.

We have a wonderful relationship now and I see her every day. We go shopping together and my husband and I have even moved house to be nearer to her. She is the only person I trust to let the baby stay overnight with and I know she respects the routines I use (she has witnessed the marvellous results!) although she is more flexible with them than I am.

Aside from my husband, my mother has definitely become my best friend and the baby loves her to bits and sees her as a second 'mum'.

A daughter who becomes a mother herself frequently finds that she can suddenly appreciate her mother's perspective on life. Many women have told me how they only realise just how much their mothers did for them once they have children to care for themselves. A friend recently told me how when her mother was dying in hospital she had held tightly on to her hand – something she had not done for many years. Even though her own children had been around for several years, this close contact bought home how much her mother had cared for her. It came to her in a huge rush how the hands she now held had seen her safely across the road; bathed and dressed her; wiped her bottom and her nose; plaited her hair for school; clapped the loudest at her school concerts and sports days; prepared thousands of meals for her; washed and ironed her clothes; and provided comfort and safety on so many occasions. The new mother finds a different perspective once she is doing all these simple things for her own baby, and it can frequently create a closer bond with her own mother.

Debbie (35):

I have a very loving and close relationship with my mother. I feel that since I have become an adult we have become closer. She has always been a very strong person, especially when she was going through a very difficult divorce. She always made sure that my sister and I came first and to a certain degree tried to shield us from a lot of her true feelings with regard to my father. I can understand now, after having a child of my own, why she did this. She would have done anything to protect us from the hurt and upset a divorce can cause.

My mother is my best friend and we have unconditional love for each other. There have been times when our roles have been reversed and I have played the mother figure to support her during difficult times. I have always tried to give my mother sound, honest advice when she has asked for it. I go to her when I want help and support and I know she always has time for me.

I have always been shown a lot of affection by my mother and I hope I can do the same for my daughter. We both agree that you should always make time for your children but also realise that time for one's self is as important. She went back to work when I started school and I am about to return to work now that my baby is one year old. She also agrees with me on the issue of children needing stimulation outside the home; she supports me and my husband taking Olivia to nursery school from such an early age.

It can take a life-changing experience to give us all a wider view of life and what the important things are. When my own mother died I found myself questioning many things about the world and my place in it. My friend, who held her mother's hand as she was dying, found comfort afterwards in continuing the pattern of simple caring as she looked after her own children. Birth is a no less powerful tool than death for encouraging reassessment and focusing on a legacy for the future.

Sarah (32) writes:

My mum had me when she was only 20 and, as a result, I think her approach to parenting is different to mine. I feel a lot more confident about being a mum and coping than my mum did, due to our different life experiences before having children. Mum lived at home with her parents for the first six months of my life and so had a network of support close by. However, when my parents got a place of their own she struggled, and developed postnatal depression. When I was pregnant I was scared that I would too, but other than the odd bad day, I have been lucky.

Mum has always been fairly relaxed and tried to be my best friend rather than my mum – and she probably is. Even now when I'm ill all I want is a cuddle from my mum and I like to share most things with her. I went through the usual teenage 'I hate you' stage, but my parents split up when I was 12 and my mum suffered from depression again, so I think I grew up very quickly. We have always been very close and never had a serious falling out over anything. I don't think we have any differences of opinion on parenting issues – Mum just lets me get on with it and offers me advice and encouragement if I ask for it. The positive influence she has had on me is that she has always been kind, loving and caring and has always been there with a kind word and encouragement when I have needed her. The negative influence I think is that some of her lack of confidence in herself has rubbed off on me and that sometimes she was too soft with me. I think I will be a tougher mum than she was, but I can only hope that I will mean as much to my daughter as my mum does to me.

Perhaps the ability to overcome the sins of the fathers – or in the case of this book of the mothers – is something we should acknowledge more in our society. For every media opinion about the deterioration of family values, the so-called end of marriage and traditional family structures there is an untold number of women trying to do a better job of raising their families than they experienced themselves. This is a profoundly positive, and therefore unfashionable, view of life. If the newspapers are to be believed we are living in an increasingly violent, irresponsible and desperate world. But for an alternative view, you only have to go along to a coffee morning for mothers of young children or to a soft play session. If you witness, as I sometimes have, the quiet love and care the children are receiving and listen to the women talking among themselves, vowing more for their children, you realise that it's in this concern for the next generation shown by mothers everywhere that the hope of society lies.

The general consensus is that what we value most in our best friends are the qualities of trust, loyalty, support and the ability to listen to us and share our anxieties. For every woman who declares that her mother is her best friend, there is one who deems her mother distant, unsupportive or downright destructive. I found that the women in the first camp have a huge amount of value added to their lives by this essential relationship with their mothers. My husband was my best friend for a decade but when he left the scene there was really only one person I could turn to. My mother's loyalty, energy and humour got me through the most difficult period of my life. The lines between mother and best friend were blurred.

Every day I am thankful for this. I remember so much of her motherly/sisterly/best friend advice to me. She was a complex person, so complex she didn't even know herself what she was thinking half of the time. But her cup was always half full – never half empty. My mother never saw life as one door closing; always as another door opening. Onwards and upwards, she would say. Her favourite quote was, 'We may be working class, but we are not working class like them next door.'

All of my life she would tell me: 'Gina, you can do anything you want and be anyone you want – but try to do it, and be it, slim and with your make-up on.'

Chapter 3

❈

Other
Mothers

❈

A few years ago I was walking around the local supermarket in the town where I grew up. I bumped into a girl I had gone to school with and whom during my adolescent years had been fairly close to. We recognised each other instantly and spent a good 15 minutes talking at a frantic pace about what we each had done with our lives since the last time we had met which was, in fact, many many years ago.

Then she touched upon my mother's death, asking how I was coping. I was honest and said that it had not been easy and although she had been dead for nearly three years at the time, I still thought of my mother on a daily basis. To my astonishment she said, 'So do I – there is rarely a day I do not think about your mother and some of the influences she has had on my life.'

I found my body going rigid as I thought: Oh, my God what's coming next? Was it the time she got up in front of all of my friends and belted out her rendition of 'Twist and Shout' in a voice as flat as a pancake? Or, even worse, the time she hauled herself on to the bare back of the local farm horse, wearing her favourite black suede three-inch-heel stiletto shoes and a skirt that was so tight she could not straddle the horse? She just lay along its back clutching for dear life as the horse bolted down the road, with her roaring and laughing her head off.

I smiled serenely, preparing myself for the worst when she announced, 'Every time I do my dishes I think of your mum and how she said it was of the utmost importance, in the interests of hygiene, that every single dish should be either dried with a clean cloth that had been washed on a 90-degree wash, or rinsed thoroughly under hot running water and allowed to air dry.' In a very serious voice, my long-lost friend announced, 'Georgina – some days I just don't have the time to do that, and leave them covered in soap suds on the drainer to dry. Do you think I could be damaging my kids by doing this?' I swear to God that I laughed so much I nearly fell head first into the ice-cream freezer.

Yet the story should not really have surprised me because over the years my mother did have a huge impact on the lives of other people's children. The cousins I grew up with and whom she used to help care for when they were young are still influenced to this day by certain aspects of life that she touched upon. Hand-washing was an obsession with my mother, which she passed on to me and several of my cousins. Washing the whites at 90 degrees and the coloureds at 40 degrees, separating light colours from dark colours is another obsession. It's one that I can't help passing on to to the many mothers who read my books. It is incredible that a woman, who led such an ordinary, simple life, has influenced so many people's lives. The day after she died I took one of my cousins to the chapel of rest to say goodbye to her. We looked down into the coffin where she lay in her favourite blue Jaeger suit and her best shoes. Her wig had been beautifully coiffured and the only thing that I had forgotten was her false teeth. Unfortunately rigor mortis had set in and, try as they might, the undertakers could not get them in.

Despite this, she looked like the mother that I had known for most of my life, not the one whose body had been racked with pain and disease for five years. She looked at peace.

As we said our farewells and I kissed her goodbye for the umpteenth time, my cousin looked at me and with tears in her eyes she said, 'She was an icon.' And indeed she was. This very ordinary, yet extraordinary, woman called Helen Jane Ford, died without realising just how much she would be responsible for changing motherhood, through her influence on her daughter.

It is not only her influence that has shaped my life but that of 'other mothers'. My two aunts have also gone a long way in determining how my career in childcare has been shaped, and in one particular way my Aunt Jean shaped and changed the course of my life.

Although she tried her best, my mother was not the best of cooks – she used to laugh and say the tin opener was her best friend. I am sure the growth of the company Heinz Foods was improved hugely by my mother. How long things should take to cook baffled her, even simple things like potatoes and carrots. A good 45 minutes after they had been put on the stove she would be staring curiously into the pan, prodding with a fork and asking my granda if he thought they would be ready yet. She would look on anxiously as my granda and I tucked into her specialities, and we always praised her efforts, no matter how grim.

But no matter how hard she tried her meals never tasted like those cooked by Aunt Jean. The Fray Bentos pies and Birds Eye trifles, washed down with fizzy lemonade, were not a patch on the wonderful homemade meals and freshly made lemonade that she used to churn out. More often than not my granda would sneak out after tea to my Aunt Jean's hoping there would be a bowl of her delicious Scotch broth left over, or some yummy rhubarb crumble and custard. Years later my Aunt Jean confessed that she always cooked for eight instead of six, to ensure that there was always some spare for my granda and me.

I used to be in awe of my Aunt Jean when she was preparing these huge meals. There could be as many as eight of us children running around the house, screaming and shouting at the tops of our voices, but she made it look so simple and in no time at all we would be sitting around the huge old wooden table. To me that was what family meals should be like and by the time I was 10 years old I took over the running of my mother's kitchen and the cooking. I got up every day at six and prepared the food that we were going to have that evening. I still have the first two cookery books I used: *The Dairy Cook Book* and the *Be-Ro Cook Book*, where I first learned the art of baking. By the age of 12, when other girls were drooling over the local youths I was drooling over cookbooks. Not only was I cooking the everyday meals, but each Sunday I had a massive baking day. Chocolate cakes, cherry cakes and apple tarts were particular favourites.

Years later when I started working as a maternity nurse I took feeding the baby very seriously. Heaven forbid that any of my babies should ever be offered a jar! A jar of baby food was tantamount to rubbish, in my eyes. If ever I worked in a house where I doubted whether the mother was going to wean her baby on to real food made with organic vegetables and fruit, I would go back when the baby was ready to be weaned and spend hours cooking and puréeing. I must have peeled tons of vegetables over the years, and the majority of the early Gina babies never had one teaspoon of processed food touch their lips. One of the things I feel most proud about in my career is the influence I have had on the eating habits of the babies I have cared for. Watching so many of them growing has been such a pleasure, particularly when I see how much they enjoy healthy food.

While it is clear that it was my Aunt Jean who led me to be passionate about feeding young children on a variety of healthy foods, only one of her daughters followed in her foot-steps by building a repertoire of recipes. The other three were certainly tending more towards my mother's style of cooking.

Cooking and providing her children with a healthy nutritious diet would certainly put my Aunt Jean in the category of 'good mother', but does that mean my mother is in the category of 'bad mother' because she approached feeding me differently? I don't think so, but I was grateful to have Aunt Jean as an 'other mother' to show me that there were other ways of doing things.

Yet it was my Aunt Mary who had the biggest influence on my teenage years. As you will probably have already gathered, my mother had a very distinct dress style. When I was growing up, I was aware that when she walked into a room she turned many heads. Her dress sense was impeccable. But, unfortunately, her idea of how a woman in her early thirties should look – smart and sophisticated – was not the ideal image of how a young girl of 14 years of age should look.

My mother could not seem to grasp that I wanted to look like all the other girls: have long straight hair parted in the middle like Marianne Faithfull, and wear miniskirts and platform shoes. My wardrobe was packed with smart little suits, dress coats and matching hats, and straight skirts with matching twin-sets. Which was not dissimilar to the clothes that hung in her own wardrobe.

The amount of tears I shed over these outfits was unreal, but she was uncompromising. There would be huge rows every week about fashion and she would say: 'But you look so smart in that skirt and twin-set.' When you're 14 years of age and spending many hours each day standing in front of the mirror singing 'Shang-a-lang' into your hairbrush along with the Bay City Rollers, looking like Audrey Hepburn does little for your self-esteem.

I had always been very shy of boys and my self-image did nothing to help me get into the boy-girl thing that all my friends seemed to be enjoying. At the local youth club parties I would sit at the edge of the room feeling so self-conscious about my appearance that when a boy actually did approach me I could do little more than mumble a few words, usually sarcastic ones, to cover up my shyness.

Aunt Mary was 10 years younger than my mother, and only 10 years older than me and I used to spend hours pouring my heart out to her. My mother thought the world of her and they became great friends the minute my uncle started dating her. Eventually, after a lot of persuasion, my mother agreed to allow Aunt Mary to take me shopping. From that moment on, it was out with the sophisticated tailored skirts, twin-sets and smart little two-pieces. In came the micro-minis, bell-bottom trousers, sexy tops and loads of shoes in fabulous bright red, lime green and orange – all with amazing platform soles. To heck that I could hardly walk in the shoes and the hemlines barely covered my bum – I got what I wanted: to look like every other kid on the block.

With that battle conquered, thanks to Aunt Mary, the next one was to allow me to start dating. This took a lot more persuading and my Aunt Mary and I had to involve at least three other mothers at a family summit before my mother would agree that I could attend my first real party, without adult supervision.

When I talk to a 14-, or 15-year-old nowadays, I am astonished at how confident and more advanced they seem than I was when I was growing up. They seem so much worldlier and many are already in their first serious relation-ship by this age. However, at that first grown-up party, although I did not feel it, with my newfound cool image I could at least put on an air of confidence. The party took place on the local beach and was attended by about thirty teenagers aged between 14 and 19. As the music blasted out of a portable radio, I was approached by the local cool guy, a biker called Dave the Rave. He was 18 years of age and had hair right down to the middle of his back, so long that it touched the bottom of his short tight leather jacket. I thought I had died and gone to heaven when this Adonis asked me if I wanted to take a walk.

As we strolled hand in hand along the moonlit beach I looked up to the stars and said a quiet thank-you to my wonderful Aunt Mary. Without a doubt Dave would never have given me a second look if I had been dressed by my mother. It was quite clear to me on that night that my mother did not have a clue about being a teenager, and I made a silent vow not to listen to any more of her advice about clothes or men in the future.

When Dave suggested that we lie down in the sand dunes and look at the stars, it was like something out of the fantastic romance magazines that I used to sneak a read at when I stayed at my Aunt Mary's. As his embraces got more and more passionate I suddenly felt his hand sneak up my skirt. It was so short that he did not have to move it very far to reach the bit that my mother had told me was totally out of bounds. As I pushed his hands away, I recall him saying: 'What's wrong? I thought you were up for it.' In a very serious voice I explained that I was *not that type of girl* and that I was saving myself until I met the right man. Within minutes he was up on his feet and legging it back to the party, muttering something along the lines of, 'What the hell are you wearing an outfit like that for if you're not up for it then?'

Confused and puzzled, I got up from the dunes and adjusted my micro-miniskirt and sexy frilly blouse, feeling a bit cross that it had got covered in sand. By the time I got back to the party Dave was already in a passionate clinch with a girl called Janice. I spent the rest of the night looking on at everyone else enjoying themselves – trying to fathom out this boy-girl thing and what exactly my mother wanted me to save myself for.

Twenty years later I met Dave the Rave in the street. The long silken hair was gone and only a few grey tufts stuck out from behind his ears. Two of his front teeth were missing, his complexion was that of an over-ripe strawberry. The one thing that remained the same was the leather biker-style jacket – only this time he had the most massive beer belly sticking out of it. It was then that I realised just what a wise woman my mother had been and how her advice on saving myself had saved me from the Dave the Raves of this world!

I was so lucky to have my 'other mothers' in those two special aunts. It goes without saying that all children are influenced by people other than their mothers. There is an important stage of adolescence where the child needs to move further out into the world, to find new role models and discover who they are – but with that parental hand still there to guide and support them. Sometimes the background figures of early childhood – the aunts, the godmothers, friends of the family – come to the forefront as a child grows up. They help to provide her with alternative approaches to life which she is hungry to learn about, even if it's as simple as cookery demonstrations and micro-miniskirts.

Mothers are not perfect and they can never provide their children with everything they need in life. Just as I turned to Aunt Jean as a domestic role model when my own mother's culinary efforts failed to please, I found in my research for this book that many women have turned to mother figures in their lives to fill a gap. The gaps are unintentional, but daughters feel a need to seek guidance and advice in many different ways. Daisy (34) told me her story:

My mother came from a very poor family. She was the oldest of 10 children living in a three-bedroom house. She had no sort of childhood at all and effectively raised the last few babies. For years my mum's youngest sister thought my mum was actually her mother. She married at 20 and quickly had my sister and me. My dad was in the forces and his job took them all over the world. She was frequently very lonely, missing her huge family and the hectic household. But motherhood was the most natural thing in the world to her and she devoted herself entirely to loving and caring for her daughters.

When I was 12, I went to boarding-school and my sister followed two years later. This was because our dad's job would make a stable education impossible and, as a grammar school boy from a middle-class background, he felt this was the most important thing to provide his children with. It broke my mother's heart. She never forgave my dad for sending us away and she never really got over losing her babies.

And she did lose us. The world I met through the vast variety of my school friends was a far cry from her world. When I returned home each holiday, the gap between my mother and me had grown wider and wider. She had had a tough life and had barely been educated herself and the academic success that came to my sister and me set us apart from her. She couldn't follow our schoolwork and although she was terribly proud of us, we had entered an unfamiliar world and it frightened her.

After I went to university I moved to London and had an exciting job that I loved. But I felt a great lack of guidance and I longed for a mother I could talk my dilemmas over with. I made a mess of lots of relationships, choosing the wrong men and living a quite extreme sort of life.

I definitely sought mother figures out constantly and found three different women, all about my mother's age, with whom I formed very close relationships. One woman is a novelist, an agony aunt and a lay preacher. She was the person I talked boyfriend problems over with. She helped me with my spiritual life as I began to ask the big questions about how life should be lived. My other dear friend was my boss at one stage and she guided my career with great care and affection. She helped me realise my strengths and built up my confidence. The third key figure in my life has two daughters slightly younger than me. She is the person I turn to over and over again in difficult times. She has also been a wonderful grandmother figure for my sons, interested in everything they do and keen to be involved with them and discuss motherhood and all its issues with me.

I feel very blessed to have these three women in my life, but also desperately sad that my mother has not been close to me. I know she would have loved me to share my worries and thoughts with her, but I always felt that she couldn't understand my life and she could show very little interest in my work. She held me in some awe and I think that my independence and confidence intimidated her. She didn't even like my cooking, which was far too fancy for her simple tastes, even though I would try and cook very simply for her when she visited.

When my parents divorced I was in my mid-twenties. Their marriage had been running out of steam for a long time, they parted amicably and Mum was exhilarated by her newfound freedom. Our relationship recovered a great deal during this time as she was happy and had the emotional space for her daughters after many years of unhappiness. We spent a lot of time together and rediscovered each other. She then met a lovely man, fell into a very romantic love affair and married him. I was delighted at her marriage but it took top priority for her and we never again found the same closeness. When my first son was born I begged her to come and visit me and help me but she felt unable to make the long journey on her own and came several weeks later, with my stepfather. I found myself cooking meals for them and not having the close time I wanted with her, to talk about the wonder of babies and the terrible shock of becoming a mother.

My mother died recently and I have turned again to my 'substitute mums' to help me through it. I love them dearly but I am left with the sad realisation that however much they help and support me, they aren't her. I only had one mother and I wish so much I could have her back.

This story makes me very sad for the mother who lost her daughter because of the different circumstances of their lives. Daisy only had one mother but thank goodness she did have others she could turn to when she needed mothering. A lack of closeness in childhood can often be remedied when grandchildren come along, as discussed in more detail later in the book. However, the biological bond and the yearning for closeness between mother and child still exist for Daisy, in spite of her mother's death.

Children frequently seek other mothers in their search for wisdom, practical experience and alternative views of the world. But what about when the need for a mother figure is thrust upon a child? When a mother dies leaving young children behind, the necessity for a replacement of some kind, even just someone to do the cooking, is even more pronounced. Very few women I spoke to who'd lost their mothers early in life had fathers who could take over the dual parenting.

Elizabeth (40) told me:

My mother died when I was seven. I had an older brother and sister and we lived in Cardiff. Ours was a small street and a very tight-knit community. All the neighbours were referred to as 'aunty' or 'uncle' and people were in and out of each other's houses all the time. After Mum died, her best friend Aunty Peg stepped into the role of mothering us. I remember taking big black bags of washing over to her house. Dad was a police mechanic and worked long hours. Aunty Peg picked us up from school and did a lot of the cooking.

No one talked to me about my mum. My dad may have talked a bit to my older brother and sister but I wasn't allowed to go to her funeral and she was lost to me. I suppose it was a post-war generation that just coped with death and got on with things. My older sister, Linda, was 15 when Mum died and she became a mother figure for me. She cooked and cleaned the house and cared for my brother and me. It's only since Linda's own daughter reached the age of 15 that Linda has begun to get over our mother's death and the effect it had on her, taking the fun out of her teenage years. She has struggled a lot with her feelings about this and has been on antidepressants and had counselling.

When I was 11, Dad remarried and I realised how much Aunty Peg had done for us in the meantime. Our new stepmother brought three children of her own when she came to live with us. One quickly married and left. Her son moved into my brother's room with him and he then left. My sister was ready to leave home too and my two half-sisters and I shared a bedroom. Aunty Lil somehow managed to fit in and take on the role my mum had fulfilled. She became friends with everyone in the street, including Aunty Peg, which was quite an achievement. She was definitely there for us and was everything she could have been. I only really appreciated all she did for us once I had children of my own. I could see what a huge thing she had taken on, especially as she raised Dad's children alongside her own, and then nursed him through illness until his death from cancer. I had sad times when I was alone and missing my mum, unable to talk about her to anyone, but having my big sister and the 'aunties' made all the difference and we were cushioned by the sheer number of well-meaning neighbours and a tight-knit community.

Mum had been in her mid-thirties when she died and I always had a feeling that I was going to die young. I think this must have rooted itself very deep. I was really determined to mother my children as best I could in their early years so that they would remember me if I died. I worked part-time when the boys were young but once I had my daughter I had a strong need to be at home for her. When I passed the age my mum had been when she died I finally began to let go of the loss I felt and my own fears of leaving my children without a mother.

Elizabeth was fortunate to live in such a tight and supportive community. Her mother's best friend effectively took on her mother's role after her death. This happened over 30 years ago and I wonder how many women today have a network of friends who could step in and raise their children if they were unable to?

In any case, not all children are raised by their biological mothers. An average of 5,500 adoptions take place each year in the UK. Entire books are written about the effects of adoption on both the parents and the child and there are many stories of happy and fulfilled relationships. Adoptive parents often long for children and are committed to giving them the best childhood they can. The need among adoptees to seek out birth mothers is quite understandable, however happy a life they may have enjoyed with their families. One conversation with an adoptee showed how strong was her urge to find her 'other mother', who in this case was her real mother.

Jane (41):

I was adopted as a baby and eighteen months later my parents adopted a sister.

Before her marriage my mother had had an extra-ordinary job as a lab technician for the doctor who developed penicillin. She was one of only six women who were known afterwards as the 'penicillin girls' and contributed to a discovery that changed history. When she married she stopped work altogether and moved with my father to what was then Ghana. He was in the colonial service and she became pregnant out there. Their life was incredibly primitive and without basic sanitation and decent nutrition. My mother pleaded with my father to return to England once she was pregnant, but he refused. At six months she lost the baby boy she was carrying and, without proper medical attention, she was left infertile.

She was a very insecure and nervous mother. As the first to be adopted I felt that I bore the brunt of her anger about the loss of her son. She used discipline to compensate for her lack of maternal instinct towards us both. The regime at home was draconian. We were never allowed to have friends over or go out – even as teenagers. Revealing clothes, high heels and earrings were forbidden. She had real problems with me as I developed breasts and became a young woman. We were not allowed to turn on the television without permission, to answer the phone or to wash our hair more than once a week (a teenage girl's nightmare). My mother was obsessed with our weight. We were never allowed to eat more than what she prepared for us. Even now she still notes whether I've put on weight and she has called my daughter, Miranda, 'fat' to her face, which has made me angry.

It wasn't a happy childhood because of the restrictions placed upon us. My mother never stopped blaming my father for the loss of her son and as adopted daughters we never felt able to compensate. As the eldest I was pressured into academic success and into sport. My sister was the 'beauty' and I was the 'brains' – labels we have never been able to lose and which have created tensions between us.

I did very well at school, probably because I was pushed so hard. At 18 I escaped to university. Not surprisingly, it hit me like a brick wall. I was utterly overwhelmed by the freedom, and by hormones, and I formed intense and frequently disastrous relationships.

When I was 32 I traced my birth mother and found her living in Australia. She had been unmarried when pregnant with me and, then in 1960s England, without the support of my birth father, couldn't face the social stigma. She later married my father, which was something I found difficult to cope with. However, I went to see her in Australia and we made a great connection. We're very close now. She has been to see me three times and we write and email each other often. She has met my daughter and my adoptive parents as well. Things couldn't be better with her now and I am so glad to have her in my life.

My sister decided not to seek out her own birth mother and this has caused difficulties between us – she felt my need to find my real mother caused her great trauma. She is happily married and the mother of three, having given up a career as a designer to care for them full-time. She's a devoted mother, possibly because of our own upbringing.

My adoptive mother is now in her eighties and quite ill. I try to keep in touch. The same dynamics are in place whenever I return home although I try to break the patterns when I can. She tolerates me now, as an adult, and I try to curb my resentment and let her get to know her granddaughter. I am constantly on the lookout for negative messages my daughter might pick up.

Now I am the mother of a daughter, I have thought very carefully about the use of discipline as well as other aspects of mothering. I have questioned what is appropriate and have been as flexible as possible with Miranda. I have tried to give her the measure of her own freedom, but created a circle of protection around her. We are very close and I feel so proud of her uniqueness. I breast-fed on demand for two years and she slept in our bedroom for a year. I didn't work at all for the first two years of Miranda's life because I felt it was necessary to be there with her. I felt I couldn't compromise in those early years.

There are, however, many aspects of my own up-bringing that I continue to put into practice with my daughter. I don't want her to grow up too quickly. My mother's own concerns with manners and not watching too much television, for example, are ones I have also adopted. I think you take what was best from your own mothering and you try to avoid the worst things. I nurture my daughter in the ways denied to me and I take the most pleasure from motherhood as I possibly can.

Every woman can reflect back on her formative years and identify the essential 'other mother' figures, whether a relative, friend of the family or a teacher. The teenage years are notoriously tough for parents. A 13-year-old is dependent on her parents for food and clothing and often still looks like a child. Just four years later that same girl is a physically developed woman who can drive, leave school and is probably champing at the bit to join the big wide world. Getting from that first point to the next is a tremendous and sometimes difficult achievement, as parents of teenagers frequently tell me. Hopefully, mothers act as role models as well as advisers and guardians of their developing children's sense of self. For some children circumstances make other mothers vital when their own are either not around any more or unavailable to them in one sense or another. It's important for mothers whose daughters are seeking out alternative aspects of life through other women not to feel threatened by this or rejected by their daughters. As the last chapter showed, they can frequently come back to you.

❈

Chapter 4

Mother Care,
Other Care

❈

My flat in Edinburgh is one of several in a building and a group of women regularly comes in to clean. They vary in age but on the whole, they are down-to-earth Scottish women, talkative, funny and no nonsense. I often get chatting to them, and when I found out that most of them had children, and some were very young, I asked them, 'Do you feel guilty going out to work and leaving the kids with someone else?'

They looked blank. 'What are you talking about? We have to work. What are we supposed to do, leave the kids on their own?'

'Well,' I said, 'a lot of the mothers I know feel guilty if they have to leave their kids at nursery or with a minder, so they can go out and work. They worry it might damage their children.'

They howled with laughter. One said, 'Ah, Gina, get real! Guilty? What are you talking about? Working's part of life, and there's nothing wrong with my kids.'

Their attitude is refreshing. They don't analyse, they just

get on and do what they have to do. They may not be ideal mothers in some eyes, but they have a lot less stress and guilt in their lives.

I was nine years old before my mother went to work. We lived on a farm, surrounded by other families, and the mothers in those families did work, either as cleaners or in the fields, picking potatoes and suchlike for the farmer. It was not glamorous – it was hard labour and not too well paid – but it was completely accepted that the women went out and did it, as well as running the family home.

My mother tried her best but it was no good. She was hopeless at hard physical work like lifting bales of hay or lugging potato sacks. She tried but every ten minutes she had to have a rest and a cigarette, and if she wasn't doing that, she was distracting everyone by gossiping and joking. Finally the farmer said if he kept her on, he'd go bankrupt. My mum just wasn't suited to that work, so she looked after me and my cousins while my aunt went out and worked on the farm, and she put a lot of energy into that.

There were times I wished my mother had something to think about other than me. Her interest in me and my life could be quite intense. I'd come home from school and she wanted to hear about and analyse every minute of my day, and she was obsessed with my appearance, wanting me to look just right. Woe betide me if my hem was down, or there was a run in my jumper or a scuff on my shoes. It was great that my mother was so interested in me because it made me feel special and loved – I knew girls whose mothers couldn't care less – but I couldn't help wishing at times that she was a bit less enthusiastic about it. Sometimes, much as I loved her,

I found it suffocating. Then, when I was nine, a local manor house was turned into an old people's home and one of my aunties got a job as a cook there. She told my mother they were looking for waitresses. My mother's first thought was that she couldn't do it, she'd never done anything like it in her life, but her sister told her not to worry, as they would provide full training. So she applied, and to her great excitement she got the job.

I remember the day she went off to work for the first time. She was so nervous and proud and full of anticipation. We all oohed and aahed over her uniform – a black dress with white collar and cuffs and daisies round the collar. Mum told me she'd never felt so smart. She put her good shoes in a bag and walked the three miles to the manor alongside the old railway track and through three fields. That night she came home full of stories of how much fun it had been, and the people she had met. She couldn't wait to get back the next day.

One of the happiest memories I have of my mother is the Friday when she received her first pay packet. She told me to come and meet her after work and I couldn't wait for school to end. It was a beautiful summer day without a cloud in the sky and as I ran along the railway track and through the three fields I was too excited to be as frightened of the cows that lived in them as I usually was. When I finally arrived, breathless and hot, my mother was waiting for me at the gates, holding her precious pay packet.

True to my mother's practical nature, we went straight to the shops and bought sweeties and fizzy drinks to take home to celebrate the rewards of her first pay packet. All the way back, she chatted away, telling me what had happened and what she'd learned. Every 10 minutes we'd stop so that she could show me the posh things they'd taught her at the manor. I laugh when I think about it now – a woman in her waitress's black dress miming how she poured the tea, to a little girl in a school uniform who hung on her every word, as they stood in a field full of cows. 'This is how you do it, Georgie, you serve from the left and clear from the right,' she'd say, or she'd show me how to fold the napkins just so. I thought she was a genius, plain and simple: a superwoman who could do anything. And she was far too excited to notice that I hadn't changed out of my good shoes and that I'd scuffed them round the tops. She was twenty-nine years old.

It changed my life and hers. From then on, I had a very positive sense of what work could be for women. My mother's struggle with ill health meant that she had suffered on and off from depression since I was born and this job gave her a new sense of purpose and happiness. I was much happier knowing that she was happier. In the years to come, work made my mother really contented, and back when she started that waitressing job, she had the benefit of knowing I was already a big girl and that on the farm where we lived there were relations who could look after me.

In most societies, children are reared collectively – they have several mother figures that they know will care for them, whether family members or neighbours. Even in British society, until the 1970s and 80s, raising children was often a shared responsibility. Many families like my own did what my mother did, and left their children with family members or paid other women to care for them; others hired nannies. Some families expected to have a nursery maid when babies came, and because families tended to stay in one area, there was usually plenty of help and support on hand. The notion that motherhood is a lone activity has coincided with the trend for families to live long distances apart.

Motherhood is an enormous undertaking, and the idea that it should be the entire responsibility of one woman seems ludicrous. If all mothers were capable of coping alone with their babies, I would never have had a job in the first place. The fact that I found myself in huge demand from the very earliest days of my career shows that many mothers are very far from being able to cope alone, and I believe they shouldn't have to. In fact, I think it is an intolerable burden to put on a woman.

Of course parents have always wanted to do the best for their child – ABC blocks to help the infant to learn his letters were introduced in the reign of Elizabeth I. The burden of the modern mother is something else, though. Once, it was enough to feed and clothe your child, to keep it clean, nurse it when it was sick, and take it to church to guarantee its future salvation and its moral health. The modern mother is faced with a baffling array of childcare theories that warn her that her job is much more than this. She is given total responsibility for the mental development and emotional stability of the child in her care; she is told that if she doesn't stimulate it adequately in its first years of life, it will suffer immeasurably for the remaining miserable years. Jean Liedloff's book *The Continuum Concept*, mentioned in Chapter 1, advocates the continuous carrying of an infant. In the 1970s, more mothers than ever were returning to work. How were they supposed to fit this continuous carrying into a job? The answer was that these jobs were often a matter of choice; the mother could, if she realised the need for her presence during the baby's first year, give up the job in order to avert the deprivation which would damage the baby's entire life and weigh her down for years as well.

This kind of pressure sank into society's consciousness. Mothers began to feel that they had a huge, almost limitless responsibility towards the child, and that they must watch every word and every action in case it scarred the growing infant. The task would be easier if we could only agree on what the right way is, but theories change all the time. One day we hear that day care is beneficial for a child's development; the next, that it will make the child grow up antisocial and aggressive. One newspaper headline tells us children must be given their independence as soon as possible, another claims that only the 24-hour presence of the mother will do. The question of whether mothers should look after their children full time or go out to work remains confused, with mixed messages coming from the government, experts and the media.

In 2000 Kate Figes in *Life after Birth* took the commonsense approach. She pointed out that many mothers work, and that the benefit to children of their mothers working far outweighed any disadvantages. She felt keenly the unrealistic pressure on women to stay at home and devote themselves to their children:

> If mothers were perfect and able to respond to each and
> every demand made by a child at exactly the right time,
> their children would grow up with severe problems relating
> to a wider world where they can never be the most

important aspect. If mothers were never separated from their children and followed every latest theory of 'good' motherhood, their children would never have the space for spontaneity, imaginative play and healthy chaos. It isn't possible or wise to create a perfect, conflict-free world where our children's needs are always paramount, because they have to grow up and live in the real world, riddled with conflict, where women work.

So who should look after the baby? And what sort of role should the state play in directing mothers' choices, or providing for those choices?

Naturally this subject is highly emotive – anything to do with the care of children always is, and with good cause. To me, it seems obvious that it is not simply a case of what is good for the child – and no one seems able to agree what that is – but also what is good for the mother. Some women wish to stay at home and be full-time mothers, many of them believing passionately that this is the only way to raise children; others long for life outside the family and feel that they would be significantly unhappy and perhaps worse as mothers if this were denied them; others have no choice and have to go out to work to keep a roof over their child's head and food on the child's plate. At the moment, 51 per cent of mothers go out to work, so the question of childcare is real and urgent. Some women can call on the help of their own mother, or mother-in-law, but the traditional fallback of Granny looking after the kids is becoming less and less of an option. For one thing, Granny might live many miles away, she might have her own job to consider or she just might not feel like caring for young children all over again, and why should she? Without the old-fashioned family networks around them, mothers have the problem of childcare to deal with alone.

Stacey (37) is a full-time mother who believes fervently that it is only by staying at home and devoting herself to her children that she can answer their needs. She has three children under seven, the youngest of whom is 11 months old. Highly educated and previously a social worker, Stacey is married to Andrew who brings home a good salary, though nothing like what their joint salary was.

When I got pregnant the first time I was convinced that I would return to work as soon as I could. I loved my job and felt I was contributing to society in a very real way. I had been to university and thrown myself into my career. But once Katie came along, everything changed. As she got older and her need for me increased, I realised that I couldn't trust anyone else to care for her in the way that I did. No matter how highly paid someone was, they wouldn't love her. It was simple for me – I didn't want her days to be spent with someone who didn't love her. It went against every instinct I had to pass her over to someone else's care while I went out to earn a wage – a wage that would mostly be eaten up by childcare costs. The only sort of childcare I could contemplate was a nanny who lived in with us. But that was way beyond our financial resources and I didn't want our new family of three becoming three plus a stranger. I went on a career break once my maternity leave was up but then I got pregnant again and the decision seemed to be made for me. I left my job for good.

I firmly believe I made the right choice. My daughter is a happier, more stable child because she has been able to stay at home with me for as long as possible. And she knows I'll be there for her every day when she gets home from school. I want her two sisters to have the same experience.

Stacey and her husband made significant sacrifices to become a sole-income family. They sold their family home and bought another in a cheaper area. They make strict budgeting a priority and rarely go on family holidays or for nights out. Stacey remembers her credit cards and shopping trips as belonging to very distant days. She does not regret the choice she's made but feels very strongly that the government, and by extension, society as a whole, does not recognise the role of women who choose to be homemakers and full-time mothers.

In fact, I've become very cynical about the whole consumer society that we seem so obsessed by. I've stopped watching the television because I couldn't bear the adverts – I just started shouting at them and that's when I knew I'd better watch out or they'd be locking me up. We're being pressured into spending money all the time on things we just don't need, at the expense of the next generation. Research has shown that working mothers spend almost all their wages on childcare, tax, commuting and the clothes and accessories they need for the office. It just doesn't make sense. The equation is ridiculous. But what really makes me furious is the government's attitude to motherhood. The whole thrust of government policy is that women should and must go out to work and pass childcare on to minders and institutions; the idea that staying at home and working to raise your own children might be valuable work and might be contributing to society by producing well-rounded, decent, hardworking citizens of the future who are creative and interesting and disciplined never seems to occur to anyone. The message is that it is a waste of your education to raise children, even though research shows that the more educated the mother, the better off her children are. And who on earth do we expect to raise children – the uneducated? Because of the government's bias against non-employed mothers and against the traditional family unit, the whole situation is iniquitous. If you are a dual-income family, you enjoy two personal tax allowances and are eligible for Working Family Credits that are denied to single-income families. In effect, you are taxed more for staying at home, when there is less income coming into the house. There is no possibility of transferring an unused tax allowance to a partner or spouse, which seems an obvious and fair thing to do. Childcare within the home is regarded as entirely your responsibility; once childcare moves outside the home, it is state-aided. That seems deeply unfair. I also have to consider my pension provisions – if I take too long out of the system I will fall behind in my contributions and will perhaps not be eligible for full benefits when I'm a pensioner, because I worked inside the home instead of out. In every way, it seems that mothers are undervalued and considered nothing by society and by the government. I fully intend to return to work when my children are old enough – and I might add that there is a crying need for social workers – so

I simply can't agree that my education has been wasted. It makes me angry and resentful that while I raise my children, I'm considered invisible by the state.

Mothers like Stacey find a fulfilment in caring for their children that conforms to our idea of what the maternal woman is like. She gains a rich emotional reward in being with her children full time. In fact, it is that picture of the unconditionally loving, deeply nurturing and self-sacrificing woman that is at the heart of society's image of what a 'good mother' is, so it is interesting that Stacey feels so undervalued and essentially invisible when she seems to be doing the 'ideal' job. She sees government policy as blindly assuming that all mothers want to work and penalising those mothers who consider raising their children a job of work in itself.

Caroline (36) is a single mother and found the early years alone with her daughter extremely hard. Like many women she suffered from depression and feelings of isolation. And like many women today, she is deeply concerned about the current attitude towards getting mothers back to work:

I don't feel that the solution to the dilemmas mothers face regarding work lie with the government. I feel angry that giving women tax breaks to encourage them back to work is seen as the only way of tackling society's problems. I feel this approach is potentially disastrous for the next generation. Responsibility does rest with government, however, for providing decent nutrition for schoolchildren and for trying to reduce the huge gap that exists between the poorest children and those from the wealthiest backgrounds. I fear that the American model of working hard in order to succeed in financial terms is a dangerous one. The atmosphere of the importance of money that exists at the moment takes away from the natural processes of life. There is a glaring lack of acknowledgement of child-centric needs, as opposed to what adults want for themselves.

Since Ellie was three I have begun working again. I am developing a career as a literacy specialist. Teaching is something I love and I have found a life for myself outside the home. Ellie is now at school part-time and I work during these hours. During school holidays I use a child-minder when I work and also when I need time for myself to go to the gym or to have some space for myself. I realised that I needed to nurture my own needs as well to be a better mother.

There are some people who see mothers who are convinced that they alone can raise their children as selfish, and at the mercy of their own insecurities. Ruth (26) said:

I don't want to put Oscar into childcare because I don't want him loving anyone else more than he loves me. It might sound silly, but I can't bear the thought of him falling over and hurting his knee and raising his arms to be picked up by someone else. I feel as though people look at me accusingly when I tell them I'm a full-time mother, as though I'm not capable of doing anything else, or I'm choosing the easy option, spending all day sitting on my bum and eating chocolate. Actually, I barely have a minute to myself and I help out with reading at the local primary school which Oscar will eventually attend. There is a national shortage of volunteers now, because mothers have given so much for free for decades. Now, they don't because they have no time and because they devote their working hours to earning money for themselves – and that's what the government encourages. The more you work for yourself, the better off you are. The more you work for others, the less well off you are. Just think of what nurses and teachers are paid as compared to lawyers and bankers. Any caring profession is regarded as the preserve of low-paid women. That is repeated throughout society. It makes me very sad.

One of the reasons why mothers choose to stay at home is apprehensiveness about day care. Some have serious concerns that care from anyone other than the mother is detrimental to a child's development, and modern research can feed this fear.

The Institute for the Study of Children, Families and Social Issues is taking part in a massive study of the effects of modern childcare, following over 1,000 children from birth to school age. In 2005, it released results that showed some negative effects of day care for children under two years old. Naturally the media leapt on these findings with glee – here was further proof that mothers who went out to work were selfish creatures who didn't mind damaging their children for financial gain. The research found that pre-school education for children over two was generally beneficial but that for children under two, there was a rise in antisocial behaviour and aggression. The message came across loud and clear – mothers should not put young children into childcare. But, as with most things, it is not that simple. The number of children who do exhibit this kind of bad behaviour is very small, and they often lose their aggressive characteristics as they approach school age. In fact, the research shows that children gain more from day care than they lose. As with most things in life, it is the *quality* of that care that matters, and that is where I believe the crux of the issue lies.

Eleanor, 37, went back to her job as the marketing manager for a leading UK charity when her first baby, Bella, was six months old. She intended to return from the moment she found she was pregnant and nothing changed her mind. She and her partner decided to put Bella into full-time nursery care.

> I've never felt guilty at all about returning to work. I knew I wanted to and that it would be right for me. Childcare is expensive, and we don't qualify for any credits or anything, so a big chunk of my earnings is spent on care for Bella. But that won't always be the case, and I will have gained enormously in every way by continuing my career. I did a lot of reading when I was pregnant and I was aware of the various attachment theories and intense mothering and things like that. And often they made sense – the carrying, for example, you can see the reasoning behind it, but in the real world, it's just not practical.
>
> I read the horror stories about nurseries, and they did give me a pang, but once I actually started looking at places I was quickly reassured. It was obvious to me that the staff were good and caring and that Bella would be safe and well looked after. I honestly feel that Bella has a better time there than she would if she were at home with me. I think it would be boring for *her* to be with me all the time,

and I would not be cut out to stimulate her properly. I feel absolutely happy with my decision. I have no qualms.

I decided to go back to work full-time because it would make me happy, and it would make Bella happy too, because I can't imagine anything worse than being stuck on your own with a miserable mother. I could never see myself as being *only* a mother. I would be a worse mother because I would resent the baby up to a point. I was interested to see how I was going to feel once I got back to work and I would have been very surprised if I'd felt bad. Thank goodness I didn't. I really liked it, and I didn't miss Bella at all. I knew I'd be seeing her that evening, so I tried not to think about her. There's plenty to keep my mind occupied at work, so it isn't difficult. People are surprised when I say I'm back at work full-time but I've never sensed any criticism, which is good because I would certainly never criticise any choice someone else made. I didn't even consider going back part-time, although other colleagues work that way. I've always observed that the part-timers seem to end up doing the same amount of work and getting paid less.

There is the stereotype of the hassled working mother, running from one place to the next with carrot in her hair and baby sick on her clothes, feeling completely stressed out and unhappy. I have to say, that's not me. It is a slog sometimes but we've worked out a routine that suits us. I do find leaving work at 4.30pm difficult because normally I might have worked until 6pm, and it's hard walking out of the office at 4.30, especially on a Friday. I'm sure I'm wrong but I have the feeling that people are thinking 'Oh!', which makes me a bit uncomfortable. I go and pick up Bella from nursery, feed her and get her ready for bed, and Alex comes in later. Because Bella's on a routine, she's in bed asleep by 7pm and we have our evening together, which is absolutely fantastic and really important for our relationship. I don't have any help at home, so I try and be organised at weekends so that we don't spend the whole time cleaning and shopping – I do almost all the shopping via Internet deliveries, which I think are fabulous.

I would find this whole thing much harder without my partner being so incredibly supportive. Patrick is very happy with our childcare and gives me no sense that I ought to be with the baby. If there had been any sign of that, I would have been shocked and frankly pissed off. As it is, he's always eager to be involved and is fine to take over the childcare for the evening if I have to go out. Although we do split the load as equally as possible, I suppose it's inevitable that there is more on my shoulders. But when Patrick is away, I miss him like mad because doing everything is very hard work, and I know how lucky I am.

I'm not really worried about whether people think I'm a good mother or not. I'm happy with what I'm doing. But I would never openly say to people that I wasn't entirely fulfilled by child-rearing, I'm not sure why. I think it's because other people are fulfilled by it, and they've made the choice to do it, and it's not boring to them. I respect that, but it's not right for me. Sometimes I feel that I must not be a very good mother because I'm happy to be hands-off and let my husband do it if he wants to but if I sit down and think about it, I feel no guilt at all because I think I'd be bored and lonely looking after Bella day after day and I think that would come across, she would realise it.

If Bella became ill or I had a baby who needed me at home, I don't know how I'd cope. It is an odd thought that you might absolutely have to change your life because of a baby, but of course I'd do that if I had to. As it is, I feel I've successfully managed to combine motherhood and work, for the moment at least. I love Bella tremendously and having her is absolutely wonderful but I'm really glad I've managed to hold on to something of my old self, and that motherhood hasn't taken me over completely.

Eleanor's well-paid work with a large charity who can afford to keep her job open, plus a supportive, helpful partner, have made her choice to be a working mother realistic and manageable. What is vital, though, is that she trusts her childcare, which she is lucky enough to be able to afford, and most importantly of all, she is doing what is right for her.

Jessica (38) has also sent her child, Tom, to nursery, but she didn't find the experience easy at all:

I am a solicitor and the main breadwinner in our family. We had our son when I was 35. We just couldn't afford it before and we had this idea that you needed to have money to have children. It took me a while to get pregnant and I hated the whole nine months. I was overweight and exhausted all the time. I worked hard and full-time until I was 36 weeks. I had planned to work until I was 38 weeks. I'd only been able to convince Max about having a baby at all by saying I'd go straight back to work afterwards. He was worried about money as he was still a student at this point and my salary was sustaining our lifestyle.

The maternity package at work was the statutory minimum. I went back to work seven months after Tom was born because I had no choice financially. I felt that my colleagues thought I had chosen a family over my career and I have not been promoted since, which is very frustrating.

Having said that, I didn't actually want to look after Tom full-time. I struggled a lot with him as a baby and I needed some adult time for myself, especially to use my brain and feel that I was more than just a mother. Two days a week would be my ideal choice, but I needed to work at least three days to pay the bills. Tom goes to a nursery. I have felt constantly guilty about this. For three years he cried every single morning when I left him. It was horrendous. On nursery days he would start to cry from the moment he woke up. I had to prise him off me at the nursery door. I was invariably late for work and often in tears myself. It prevented me working properly. When I picked him up he was exhausted and tearful. He would be in bed an hour after he got home because he was so shattered. I had no real quality time with him at all. My job demanded I work extra hours sometimes and I just couldn't cope. After a year of this everything spiralled out of control. I went off sick from work and the doctor signed me off with stress for six months. I was on antidepressants. My husband was working long hours, my parents are a long way away and it was the toughest time of my life.

I was surprised to find I got lots of support from other

women at work. It seemed I wasn't the only one trying to juggle a career and motherhood. Once I'd admitted I was struggling, other women came forward to tell me their problems, which really helped. I felt ready to go back to work after six months and we tried a new childcare plan to avoid going back down the depression route again. I now work four days a week and look after Tom on the fifth day. Tom is in nursery a day and a half. Max changed his job so he could look after him for a day and a half. On the fourth day, Max's mother looks after him as she has moved nearer to us now. This works so much better for everyone, although I do struggle with Granny a bit, as she has no rules or discipline at all for Tom when he's at her house. But I can't complain, on the whole.

Now that Tom is happier and going into nursery with enthusiasm each day, I've started to think about a second child. I just couldn't contemplate it before as I was so stressed from rushing about everywhere and trying to be everything to everyone. I have only just regained my status at work and fear that another baby would put me back years. We've also never been able to consider another baby while paying for nursery care. I feel it's inordinately expensive. Our monthly mortgage payment is the same as our childcare bill and we just couldn't afford to pay for two children. We've had to wait until Tom was three before even considering another baby. A subsidised crèche at work would be the best scenario for me. My profession is dominated by men, however, and change is slow. It seems to be on its way though and I'm trying out a new working from home package at the moment.

Amy (35) couldn't contemplate nursery care:

> I felt that it was my instinct telling me to stay home with my children. It seemed right to me that very young children should be at home with their mothers, having one-to-one care. Nurseries strike me as institutions where it's just not possible for every child to have the care and attention of someone who loves them. I've made the choice to stay at home and work from there. I appreciate that I'm lucky because I can work from home but we have had to adjust our lifestyles to having less money coming in. I just feel that when you're at home with your child you have literally hundreds of opportunities every day to teach them things, to get to know who they are and to build up the security that they will need to head out into the world later on. Not least of all, there are hundreds of chances to show and tell them that they are loved, and that seems like the most important thing to me. How could a nursery care worker, however lovely and good at the job, show them that?

Another mother, Olivia (36), had a bad experience of nursery. She told me that her child was 'traumatised' by the experience.

> When my daughter reached nine months, I liked the idea of a nursery for her. I thought it would give her the chance to get to know other children and have some structure to her day. I couldn't seem to manage all the messy stuff at home and I was impressed by the facilities on offer to the children at my local nursery. I thought it would be fun for her and that she would learn more than I could teach her

at home. But it didn't work out like that at all and after a while, I couldn't bear the frightened look on her face when we got in the car to go there. Although she never cried when I left her there, she would go silent on the journey and I could feel the anxiety coming off her. She was frightened by the noise of a room full of children, no matter how caring the nursery staff were. I persisted for a while but my own anxiety built up too. I watched to see if she was getting used to it and enjoying it more but as her unhappiness palpably increased I realised the mistake I was making and whisked her home for good. We were both so relieved!

Clare (39) found the idea of nurseries unappealing and followed the route of finding a childminder to help with childcare. Even this wasn't ideal, however, and she and her husband adapted the childcare arrangements for their consecutive children:

I was 27 when I had Billy and I was doing my teaching degree at the time. I had to go into college for a few hours each week and I found a childminder for Billy. I felt I was almost a full-time mum – which I wanted to be – but I was very lucky that I could continue my studies. The childminder was local and it worked very well, probably because it was only a few hours a week. Billy was nearly two when I graduated but I started straight away on my MA. At about that time Isaac was born and I only had one day a week at the university so they both went to the same childminder then. It was not an easy decision to make and I never found leaving them easy. Once I began working in a school Billy was at primary school. The childminder didn't seem right for Isaac any more as he was older and needed more stimulation, so he went to nursery while I worked part-time.

I was under financial pressure to work but I really love teaching. I also love being a mother and I found there was no such thing as having the best of both worlds. I had twin girls several years later and took two years off to be at home with them. Partly this decision was the exhaustion of having two babies and two older children to look after but we worked out that if I went back to work the cost of childcare would be more than I would earn. I missed working in those years and having another part of myself. Since the twins reached two I've gone back to work part-time gradually. My husband decided to go part-time too and we have now found the ideal solution where we both work and both care for the children. The burden of organisation and guilt doesn't fall on just one person and the children have the best of both their parents. It has taken us four children, however, to get it right! We were always aiming at a set-up like this; it's just taken a long time to get there.

The use of childminders tailed off in the wake of a few isolated incidents of mistreatment and death during the 1990s but it is now on the up again. People seem more confident again in trusting minders and like the smaller, more homely environment for their young children.

For some families, like Clare's, the answer lies in sharing the work and the childcare responsibilities. For other families, a role reversal can work very well. These days there are more fathers than ever who choose to stay at home while their wives become the main breadwinners. Jon (40) stays at home while his wife works.

> The strange thing is that lots of women tell me I must have an easy life. I find that really odd. I do all the housework, cooking and childcare and it's really bloody tiring. I'm surprised women who know what it's like seem to consider me a bit of a wuss.

While modern men are far more likely to share childcare than their fathers were, and to seek out opportunities to contribute, it is still fairly rare for the man to be the primary carer, or for men to work in early childcare. It is still seen very much as the preserve of women.

Which means that to many women, the message seems stark. You have two choices – stay at home or go out to work. A third option of working from home depends on finding the right skills to use in this way and necessitates space at home – and a lot of discipline. Women are constantly questioning which the right choice is, which is best for themselves and for their children. It can make the burden of guilt too much, not only for the woman who must work for financial reasons, but also for the woman who needs to get out of the home for her own sanity. To my mind, this pressure is not right. What is right for the mother, and fulfils her need to look after her children and have a life outside the home in whatever guise she needs or wants to, is indisputably best. Dr Catherine Hakim of the London School of Economics has published a study of this very issue, *Work-Lifestyle Choices in the 21st Century*. Questioning a large number of women and considering a huge range of statistics, she found that 20 per cent wished to stay at home full time, 20 per cent wished to devote themselves to work full time, and the majority, 60 per cent, wanted to find a work–life balance that allowed them to do both. This might sound obvious, but it is amazing how ingrained into society's mind it is that you are either a working mother or a home-bound mother. Slowly, we are being forced to change our attitudes because of the overwhelming desire of mothers that this should happen. A general shift in society is noted in research by the Future Foundation: away from high-pressured, materialistic success and towards a balance in life that has more emphasis on happiness. In their survey of 4,000 18–44-year-olds, the Foundation discovered that the majority want fulfilling jobs that interest them, which they could balance with an enjoyable life. But why is this so difficult for mothers to achieve?

Part of the problem is that genuinely fulfilling, well-paid part-time work is extremely hard to find. If you are lucky enough to work for an employer that considers its workforce imaginatively and looks to the long term, you may be able to negotiate hours that allow you that elusive work–life balance without penalising you financially and consigning you to the shelf of the has-beens and the hopeless. Eleanor's observation that if she'd gone part-time she would have done the same amount of work but for less money is a pithy one. Because of misguided notions of 'presenteeism' – if you are at your desk, you must be working – and productivity – if you're in the office from 8am until 7pm, you must be doing more than the person who is there from 9am till 4pm – part-time and flexible work is regarded almost as an admission of failure in your career, at least to some of the women I've talked to. They feel very strongly that once they became pregnant, they were forced to take a back-seat at work and made to feel that they'd made their choice about what was important in their lives. They no longer felt they were being considered for promotion or regarded as the high-flyers they once were. The fact is that 78 per cent of part-time workers are women, and part-time workers are the least well paid in our society.

Davina (35) seems outwardly to have the perfect solution to the problem. She works from home as a website editor, and her husband runs his own legal advice business from home. They share the care of their five-month-old daughter, Holly.

My dad was in the RAF and often away from home when I was growing up. I wanted Holly to have a lot of time with her dad as I felt I missed out on that. I think we're extremely lucky because we're managing to bring up Holly together. Mostly we see eye to eye on how to do it, but we have to discuss things a lot more than we would if it was just me doing what I thought was best. It's hard to manage work schedules sometimes because Pete and I both work from home. There are arguments about whose deadline is the most pressing and phone calls come in for both of us sometimes, which have to be dealt with. We're getting better at it as time goes by and we try to separate the day into chunks when one of us works and the other looks after Holly. We have lovely mealtimes together most days, though. We are lucky too that we can each choose to work in the evenings or at weekends so that afternoon trips can be taken as a family during the week as well as at weekends.

The downside of working at home means that I'm constantly surrounded by the things that need doing, like the washing up and the laundry. I will often work for an hour then rush off to hang out the washing. It can be hard to concentrate for the time I need. Pete and I argue sometimes about the housework too as I'm tidier than he is.

I love my work and couldn't bear the idea of not having it in my life. I get a sense of satisfaction when I've done a good job, which is different from the satisfaction of tucking Holly up in her cot at the end of the day. We would like to have more children, but I don't know if we'd be able to sustain the same set-up as we have with Holly. With childcare costs being so high we may have to wait until she's funded through pre-school before we can even consider another baby.

What interests me when I'm working with and talking to educated, working women who are making choices about how they will manage their lives, is their confidence. I expected that many of them would feel under pressure to 'use' their education, but instead they often feel that education is an end in itself, and that taking some years out to raise children does not mean their education has been wasted, or that by doing this they have come to the end of their working lives. They see their work as flexible, adaptable and capable of change to suit the circumstances that will make them happy. They do not feel it is anti-feminist to want to raise their families or to spend some time at home. On the contrary, they fully expect, as part of their equality and their liberation as women, to be able to do this without being penalised. The women in this position are very fortunate indeed. All they really need is for the working world to change to fit their intelligent, far-sighted approach to work and family.

The women who are the unhappiest are those who have no choice at all in how they live their lives. These are women who don't see their work as a 'career' or find it fulfilling, and who perhaps are only marginally better off working than they are on benefits. Mary (32) is typical of those women I've spoken to.

I hear about how women today have to decide about their careers and their children and feel that none of it applies to me. I have no choices about my working life and my home life because I have been a single mother since my daughter was a year old. I have to work full-time to support us both. I work long hours in a shop for a low wage because I don't have any other option. My sister looks after my daughter for two days a week and my friend for another two days. She has a subsidised nursery place for the other day. I'm lucky to have help and don't know how I would cope without it. But I am missing out on these precious years and sometimes I feel that other people are bringing up my daughter. On the hardest days I think life would have been easier if I'd never had her. It makes me so sad. The future doesn't seem very bright either. When Della starts school I will welcome schools providing day care from early in the morning until 6pm, because that will make my life easier.

It is obvious that Mary's sense of having no other options is part of what has made her unhappy and angry. A lot of women are rejecting the notion of having children at all when they have to make that choice between work and family, and the birth rate in Europe is plummeting. The governments in France and Estonia have encouraged mothers by paying them to stay at home and raise their children. In other European countries, nursery places for all children have encouraged working women to have babies. It seems that, one way or another, women may now have to be offered incentives to start a family. So what does the government in the UK plan to do to offer more choice to women?

Most measures concentrate on extending parental leave and allowances, and building up the provision of day care for young children. Current government plans include increasing the childcare element of the Working Tax Credit so that they can cover up to 80 per cent of childcare costs. They promise pre-school education places to all three- and four-year-olds, for four hours a day, 38 weeks of the year, with an increase in the flexibility of how parents can use these hours, and, by 2010, children's centres that will connect group-based and home-based carers and provide wrap-around childcare from 8am to 6pm all year round. There are plans to extend paid maternity leave from six to nine months, and then further to 12 months, and there are long-term goals to increase the educational standards of early-years child carers.

This is all laudable stuff and we must be grateful that the government is finally turning its attention to the situation of families in the modern world. But is it enough? The Day Care Trust, a charity dedicated to working for better childcare provision, doesn't think these measures go far enough and is lobbying for more care – for an increase in the hours of care guaranteed to mothers, for more funding and for the highest possible quality of care extended to all children from whatever age they go into day care. Susan Crane, its Chief Executive, says: 'High quality early education and care is crucial for children, as it affects their everyday experiences as children and can give a real boost to their learning and their social and emotional development. It is vital that early education and care is accessible and affordable, so that parents have real choices about how best to balance work and family life.'

I certainly agree with these sentiments, and I can't think of many people who wouldn't. But there are numerous factors to take into consideration. The government seems to want to fit families and working women into employment patterns that already exist, which makes life difficult for some working mothers and for small businesses. Instead, they could encourage employers to think differently about how they employ people and the investment they make in them. There is a risk that, despite all the measures the state takes, women's choices are actually being limited. After all, with millions of pounds poured into day care, the pressure will be ever greater to put children into full-time care while mothers work. Extended maternity leave and parental allowances can even prove detrimental to women's interests when small companies see women of child-bearing age as a liability and so do not wish to employ them. Some employers, particularly in small businesses, have come right out and said that they won't hire women who are likely to have children, because they cannot afford to give them the maternity rights they are entitled to.

With the government planning to extend paid maternity leave to one year, this problem could well worsen. Legislation meant to liberate the family could in fact imprison women further by reducing their options even more.

Scandinavian countries are often held up as a model, with their generous provision of childcare and their long maternity leave. We are encouraged to look to them as countries that have got it right as far as working women are concerned. But the reality may be different. Dr Catherine Hakim, in *Work-Lifestyle Choices*, points out that there is a pay threshold in Nordic countries: below it are 80 per cent of all women and above it are 80 per cent of all men. Other statistics make equally depressing reading. One is that 75 per cent of Swedish women are employed in the public sector – traditionally less well paid – and 75 per cent of men work in the private sector. Dr Hakim believes that this is because private employers have made it a policy to avoid employing women who might require some of the government's generous and expensive maternity packages. This is bad news for equality and for the situation in Britain, where the government looks set to bring in similar measures and perhaps cement women's position as second-class citizens. Interestingly, in Sweden there has also been a low take-up of paternity rights, despite incentives for men to do so.

There is nothing simple and obvious in the discussion of how women should look after their children and combine childcare and work, except that we haven't got it right quite yet. What is most important is that we do not deprive mothers of their choices by trying to imagine the perfect working mother and directing all government strategies and measures towards meeting her needs. Sometimes I feel that we need to go back even earlier in women's lives and start reshaping our expectations of how we approach education and work from the very start. After all, the traditional model of school, university and the 40 years of dedicated career that followed is one created to suit men, not women. Women have tried to slot into it as best they can. I spoke to Janet, who made me think again about the way we have accepted that this is the only way to do things. A mother and grandmother, Janet (63) is a senior partner in a law firm. She left school at 17, married quickly and had had her two children by her early twenties.

I had a sketchy education and ended up leaving school with just a typing diploma. I had a receptionist's job for a while, but in those days women often didn't intend to work for long before getting married and having a family. I was pregnant at 20 and very happy about it. No one questioned my choice then and I loved bringing up my sons while I had plenty of energy and enthusiasm. When my sons were at grammar school, my husband encouraged me to go back to school, something I had begun to think about, as the boys got older. I took some A levels, then did a Law degree at the local university. I was nothing like the other under-graduates, but I felt I brought something different to the course and I certainly worked harder than many of them! One of my sons and I took our exams at the same time, which I must admit was quite stressful! I loved my studies though and knew that I would not have been able to take on such a challenge at the age of 18. I had a year off before taking my Law Society finals and was offered articles at a local firm of solicitors. I specialised in family law and loved every aspect of my work. By this time my children had left school, travelled for a while and were each about to leave for university themselves – one to medical school and the other to law school. I think they saw my achievements as something normal and fulfilling. There were many younger women at work, but I knew I had determination and life experience to bring to the job. It was so exciting and I gradually moved up within the firm where I'm now a senior partner. My career has been very rewarding and I could give it my full attention because I had got my sons off to a good start and felt it was now 'my time'. Sometimes I feel sorry for my daughters-in-law who have had to follow a much more rigid path of school, university and career while fitting their children around it. I was lucky to have two separate aspects of life to focus on at different times.

I don't advocate all women having children in their twenties; my point is that there are different and equally successful ways of doing things. In the long term, society's attitudes to work and careers need to change: after all, we're expected to work until we're in our late sixties these days. With a working life lasting some 50 years, who is to deny anyone, men or women, mothers or fathers, the right to take some of those years for themselves, whether it is to raise their children or trek to Timbuktu?

But, whether we change our attitudes or not, childcare is a reality and a necessity. It is obvious that there must be plenty of high-quality, affordable options that allow women to work in the way they want and need to.

We must begin to value the whole task of raising children,

no matter who does it. Caring for children is one of the most important jobs there is, and we should reward the people who do it with decent pay and respect. At the same time, we must pressure employers to begin to see their workforce imaginatively, as a long-term investment that pays dividends.

'I'm a better worker now,' says Eleanor. 'I'm more organised because I have to be. I'm more driven because I've got a child at home who depends on me. Motherhood has made me more valuable to my employer, in my opinion. I'm so lucky in the childcare I have. I have complete confidence in it and know it is the best option for my daughter. I just wish that everyone could have that choice. I know it would relieve many women of the crushing guilt they feel when they go out to work.'

We only have so much energy in our lives. It is up to women today to use whatever energy they can to put pressure on the world around them – whether that is the government, their employer or their family – to make changes which will suit them and their children.

Chapter 5

❀

Mothers

at

War

❀

I n Western society, the idea of new motherhood is encap-sulated by the images of the Virgin Mary with her Child – serene, protective, content and loving. It's an image that is constantly reproduced in paintings and statues and is woven into the fabric of our cultural understanding. There is a sanctity in new motherhood, as personified by the Madonna and Child, which still represents many people's thoughts of mothers and newborn children.

We elevate new motherhood, and it continues to command a degree of interest that is, at times, surprising. You only need to look at the magazine covers on a newsagent's shelf in order to see the interest it encourages. Photographs of dreamy-looking celebrities proudly showing off their new babies gaze back at you from these magazines. Some of the weekly photographic magazines launched in the 1990s have built their success on the new offspring of photogenic television stars and other people in the public eye. The public seem to have an insatiable appetite for reading about famous women's birth experiences and impressions of life with a new baby. The articles invariably depict new motherhood as life changing and extraordinary.

The new mother is generally photographed with a caption noting how fabulous she looks despite the fact that she gave birth four minutes earlier! Most interviews reveal how wonderful and spiritual the birth experience has been, and fail to mention any epidural or Caesarean trauma. I think it's very sad that celebrities aren't allowed by the media to claim the safe arrival of their new baby as being a deeply moving experience if they didn't have a natural birth. The birth of a baby for anyone is largely a joyful occasion, whatever the baby's method of arrival. Often women have interventionist birth for reasons beyond their own control, and it's yet another thing that so many people feel a right to pass judgement on. It's almost as if society conspires to portray new motherhood in the most glorious light possible, air-brushing the reality into lovely, styled pictures of prettily made-up mothers and sleeping infants.

Motherhood is seen as a life-changing sisterhood, trans-forming lives and opening new horizons. It's as if being a new mother imbues one with a sainted quality, which is quite at odds with some of the aspects of motherhood one finds below the surface.

For while no one would deny that motherhood does have a life-changing quality, it also brings out some of the most competitive and astonishing characteristics of human nature. Behind the veil of new motherhood some women unleash their emotions in pretty unnerving criticism and competition, and direct these at none other than their fellow new mothers. One of the biggest surprises that has met the mothers I have spoken to is the rather less than supportive attitude of some of their fellow mothers.

One of my own first memories of two mothers having a lively spat was of my mother and my Aunt Jean during a wallpaper-hanging session. It all started off very well. My four cousins and I were dispatched to the back room to play and told not to disturb them until lunchtime. As we played away happily with our board games and colouring books, the two women were chatting nineteen to the dozen, deciding which part of the room they should start in and whether the paste was the right consistency. Even at the age of 10 I could sense that something was about to go wrong when I heard my mother saying: 'No, Jean, a bit more to the left. No! Up an inch. No! Not as far up as that.'

Trying to hang wallpaper covered in red roses on the walls of a cottage that were anything but straight was not the most brilliant of choices – but then practicality was never my mother's strong point. Peeking through the crack of the door I could see my aunty perched up the top of the ladder in a lilac floral pinafore and sensible flat pump shoes. My mother was standing across the other side of the room in her black, pencil-slim skirt, crisp white blouse with a perfectly starched Peter Pan collar, and around her 18-inch waist a broad bright red patent leather belt that matched her impossibly high red heels and, of course, her bright red lipstick. Immaculately made up as ever, my mother looked more appropriately dressed for an evening out rather than home decorating. As I watched her arms pointing this way and that way and instructing my aunty on the best wallpapering technique, their dialogue went something like this:

'We have to get it right, Jean.'

'For God's sake, Lena, it's only a quarter of an inch out, nobody will notice.'

'Well, I will notice, so you'll have to take it down and we'll have to start again with a fresh length – I can't have it going up not right.'

My aunty's face would be getting redder and redder. My cousins and I just knew that all hell was about to be let loose. She was yelling: 'I'll take it down all right, and the next damned bit you can put up yourself. Get your coats, kids, we're going home.'

Within minutes there was a loud slam of the door as I ran to the window and watched my aunty marching my four cousins quickly down the road. My mother was muttering in the background:

'I'll bloody well do it myself. I should have had more sense than ask Jean – she never did have an eye for detail.'

My mother was standing on the bottom rung of the ladder with a freshly pasted roll of paper hanging over one arm, and trying to balance herself with her other hand as she attempted to scale the stepladder. Try as she might she could not get further than the first step. As she stood rigid screaming for my granda – 'Dad, come quick, I'm having a dizzy turn!' – I can remember trying to fathom out in my child's brain why on earth she was trying to climb up the steps in such a tight skirt and with three-inch stiletto heels. Anyway, my mother was rescued from the stepladder and lots of tea and sympathy were administered by my granda to his very precious and only daughter. My mother's dizzy turns went on for a further couple of days, during which time Aunty Jean was persuaded by

Granda to come and help 'poor Lena' get the wallpaper up. And, God bless my aunt, as on many occasions over the years when these spats happened, she came back and the room did get finished. Each and every strip was matched to my mother's perfecting standards – a miracle, considering the crooked walls.

In the years to come on special days my mother and I would sit in the room listening to her favourite records eating meringues and drinking lemonade. She would say not once but hundreds of times, 'Always remember, Georgie, that if a job is worth doing, it's worth doing well – always do it to the best of your ability.' Those words have lived with me all of my life.

I spent most of my childhood years on a small farm in the Scottish borders. There were seven cottages on the farm and families occupied five of them. Although the families would come and go over the years, on average there were always around five sets of parents and many children living within this small community. My Aunt Jean and Uncle Dan lived in number one with my four cousins. I lived in number six with my mother, grandfather and later my stepfather, who came to live with us when I was nine. During that time I witnessed many spats and sometimes mega-rows between the mothers, but it was never done with malice or in a vitriolic way. I remember questioning my mother about how quickly these rows blew over. I was confused – one day we were being told on no account to talk to the McGlashan family again, and the next Mrs McGlashan and my mother were enjoying a cup of tea and a chat. My mother explained:

'Oh Georgie, don't be daft – so and so didn't mean it, it was like God bless you.'

I was never convinced that the God my mother referred to

was the same one that the preacher at my strict Sunday school was talking about. As the years went by I did begin to understand that within our close-knit community arguments were inevitable. Everyone's lives were so intertwined. And for every time that there was a spat between mothers it would be followed by not just one good turn, but several. These women worked together and raised their children together. They supported each other when they needed it, sometimes quietly and always unfailingly.

Mothering was something that they each went about in different ways, and while there might be disagreement about the way one or the other of them had done something, child-rearing did not feature high on the list of topics of conversation. It was just something that they got on with. For most of the time they took it for granted that what their mothers or aunties or older members of the family advised was the right way to do things.

Like the majority of women in those days, those on the farm had learned their mothering skills from their mothers and other women within their extended family. Forty years ago feminism was only beginning to impact on the well educated or the unusually rebellious. The majority of women would leave school, perhaps going on to teacher training or secretarial college. But, on the whole, the job was really just a stopgap until the right man came along, which would be quickly followed by marriage and children.

Whilst many women did return to work part-time after they had children, it was usually when the children were older and nearing school age. The main role of most women in those days was still that of wife and mother – that was considered her job, and for the majority the only job often for many years. Then along came the likes of Shirley Conran and Germaine Greer beating the drum of women's liberation and declaring that woman could have it all: higher education, university and a high-powered career. The worlds of business, banking, law, media and the like opened their doors to admit more women. As they struggled to compete with men and climb up the power ladder, the thought of having children was delayed longer and longer. We're now at a point in time where the average age for a well-educated woman to begin having children is her early to mid-thirties, as opposed to her early twenties a couple of decades ago.

The impact of these changes on the lives of today's mothers has been discussed at length in this book. When I was growing up on the farm the women didn't talk much about mothering which is why it astonishes me when I talk to mothers nowadays just how high mothering and child-raising are on the conversation agenda. And hand in hand with conversation comes competition. This seems to start during pregnancy and continue after the birth. Melissa (31) told me about her experience:

> When I was first pregnant my husband and I left the city where we'd met and married and moved out to the country. We thought the country would be a better place to raise a family and we had 'Good Life' ambitions to grow our own vegetables, etc. I never imagined how lonely I would be once we had got to our idyllic country cottage. No amount of roses growing round the door made up for the long days of my pregnancy when I was supposed to be making the

house perfect and doing some freelance work. I remember that I spent a lot of time talking on the phone to my old friends.

Once I'd registered with the local midwife she put me in touch with the organisers of some antenatal classes. I was so excited about meeting fellow pregnant women and couldn't wait to go along. It was disappointing at first, of course, because my hopes were too high and I didn't really find any immediate 'best friend contenders'. However, I loved the times in the classes when we were free to talk to each other. Soon we were comparing levels and violence of morning sickness, amount of Gaviscon consumed and pooling all our knowledge on the mysteries of birth that lay ahead. It became clear quickly who the 'natural birthers' were. One woman was hiring a birthing pool at home. I felt a bit inadequate straight away although I hadn't got very far planning the birth. It made me question myself. Then there were the comparisons between the husbands! One woman's husband was bursting with enthusiasm for the birth, he was straight down on the floor practising positions and panting while my husband sat in a straight-backed chair, cross and bored.

We all went on to have our babies in our own way and we still meet weekly four years later. Of course the comparisons have continued. Who's walking first, who's talking? My son was a bottom-shuffler and didn't walk until 20 months. By this time my friends' children were not just walking, but running, climbing and jumping. I thought that they were all feeling sorry for me for having such a delinquent child! I took pleasure in the fact that he was talking much better than their children and convinced myself that talking was much more impressive than walking anyway and proof that he was cleverer and more interesting. I suppose I was countering the competition I imagined with my own competition – one that I could win!

It wasn't competitive in a horrible way, though. Most of us were a long way from family and we needed each other's friendship. I had lots of old friends with children, but only my antenatal friends were going through exactly the same stage at the same time as me. In the early days it was an invaluable support and we took turns to cry in each other's kitchens most weeks. I think we are very lucky. Certainly our children are lucky to have grown up as friends. Three of us have new babies and have shared their arrival and the ensuing chaos of having two. Between our group, in the past four years, we've shared a marriage break-up, cancer, death of a parent and miscarriage along with the usual traumas of tantrums, potty-training and fussy eating.

I know that I have used my friends' experiences to help me work out my own style of parenting. It's not competitive in a negative way but I can see how easily that could happen.

Lots of women I've worked for have used the antenatal group as a support network. They have left their jobs, albeit temporarily, and it can be a huge shock suddenly to be alone all day with a baby rather than in the busy workplace with colleagues and friends. On the other hand I've worked for women who dismiss the whole thing, declaring they're too busy mucking out the horses.

Melissa's experience of the endless comparisons mothers make between themselves and their children is evidence of the 'good mother' complex I am trying to address. We will see later that the competitive attitudes to birth, with natural childbirth seen as the pinnacle of a good pregnant mother's aims, continue into breast-feeding and weaning. When you are surrounded by people doing it differently, it's hard to hang on to your confidence and pursue your own route through the minefield of decisions that motherhood brings. If women didn't make these comparisons they wouldn't be human: it's when the questioning becomes self-doubt and self-criticism that it causes me concern.

The group of new mothers that meets regularly can be a tremendous source of support. But what of the old friends? Women tell me over and over again how important their friendships with one another are, however close they are to their husbands. And the thing about motherhood is that it can be terribly isolating. So many of the women I have worked for found that the arrival of the baby put an end to their social life, distanced them from friends and cut them off from the world outside. As Anne Enright writes in *Making Babies: Stumbling into Motherhood*, 'Sometimes it is a lonely business. No, always. It is always a lonely business.' Women need their friends more than ever after a baby arrives, but the arrival can throw the balance of a friendship, especially where the circumstances between the friends are different. Anouschka (35) told me:

I met Elspeth about 17 years ago in my first year of university where we shared the same halls of residence. For most of the year we walked past each other, saying a brief hello, but towards the end of the year – just as we were all finding housemates to move in with – we met properly via a mutual friend of ours.

So five of us moved into a shared house together. Over the next two years Elspeth and I became very close. We started studying together, going out together and going to the library together, even though I was studying Engineering and she was studying Law. After our Bachelor's degree, I decided to do a Master's and as she also needed a place to stay for her final year of Law, we got another flat together. We had a lot of fun.

This was the year I met my boyfriend (later to be my husband). She and he also got on very well together, and although Robert and I had decided to live together, I never lost touch with Elspeth and we continued to be great friends as we found jobs, and new places to live. Once we started working we met for lunch every few days, gossiping and chatting. I remember not managing to get back to work sometimes, and ending up in a bar. I think they were the best years of our friendship together.

Once I got married to Robert, we bought a house and decided to start a family. Two years later our baby girl, Ananya, was born. She was adorable, and as we were the first in our circle of friends and family to have a baby, we had loads of visitors. Elspeth came round a lot, and became very fond of my baby. By this time she had also met a nice guy and they decided to move into a house just a few minutes away from our own. I was delighted. Imagine, we would see even more of each other! She got married and bought her house, and we saw a lot of her.

When Ananya was about a year old, I found I was expecting again (unexpectedly). Elspeth reacted in a very strange way: 'Well, that's a bit quick'. I was a little taken aback, but didn't think much more of it. Soon after, my baby boy Aidan was born. He was really different from Ananya. She was always very happy, easy to feed and eager to finish her bottle very quickly. Aidan however was very hard to deal with. He was very unhappy. He screamed and vomited a lot and was impossible to settle. I was frantic with the stress of this unhappy little fellow, and also having to deal with my 21-month-old Ananya, who was beginning to enter the terrible twos. I lost touch with so many friends during this period.

Elspeth also began to come over less and less. She blamed her job. After a little while she told me she was not well, and she was having investigative treatment in hospital. Although I knew she wasn't well, I was still under immense stress, having found out that Aidan had gastro-oesophageal reflux. The medicines weren't helping and I felt myself sinking deeper and deeper.

One day Elspeth called me and told me she was pregnant. Despite us not seeing each other for the last few months, I told her how utterly delighted I was for her. But she started withdrawing again. I was really confused, but on the other hand I had so much to deal with at home, I didn't really want to deal with this also.

She then had a beautiful little girl, Lucy, whom I didn't see, because every time I phoned Elspeth she told me that she was too busy with her family. I was so upset with her, because I didn't understand why she didn't want to see me any more. It was bewildering and hurtful.

I then found out via another friend that she was upset with me because I never asked her how she was doing any more and obviously didn't care about her when she was ill and pregnant. After everything I had been through with Aidan, who was by now recovered, I was just gobsmacked. I rang her and told her my side of the story: that I had no time to even think about myself, let alone my friends, and she told me she understood and we made up. With time, wounds do heal. We are back on speaking terms and see more of each other. I hope that, in due course, our friendship will recover completely and we will be great friends again. I think this feeling is mutual.

Anoushka's story is not unusual. When women 'join the club' of motherhood, the friend or sister not yet there can feel excluded and less important to the new mother. All of a sudden, there is a huge difference between the lives and lifestyles of two friends. The one with the baby will be less able to make the weekly session in the wine bar or the long Saturday shopping and lunch outings. The baby-free friend may find her old friend's conversation bewilderingly dull if all she talks about is sore nipples and teething. Of course, true friendships can survive and even be enhanced by motherhood for one or both friends. I know women who have been thrown together by having babies the same age and then discover a wealth and depth of friendship that can last a lifetime.

Sometimes it's not just female friends who fall out when a baby arrives on the scene. In families there can be terrible tensions between sisters, sisters-in-law and cousins. As most families are matriarchal at heart, there is a status attached to motherhood. The wayward young woman can distress her parents for years, but when she achieves motherhood she is accorded respect and admiration and the bad old days are put behind her as she ascends the family ladder. Along with respect, however, can be found jealousy and suffering.

Elsie (42) told me her story:

I fell in love with Mike when I was 23. We spent a lot of time with his brother, Eddie. We had lots of fun together and were all very close. Eddie had a girlfriend for a while, whom Mike and I really liked. They broke up and Eddie was pretty gutted. So we were delighted for him when, a few months later, he met a new woman at work. We invited Eddie and his new girlfriend, Laura, for dinner and all got on very well.

Things began to take an ugly turn when Mike and Eddie fell out about money. This was completely unlike them and, families being what they are, Laura was suspected of being behind it. It seems a bit petty now, but at the time Mike was very hurt. We didn't speak to Eddie and Laura for a while after that. But then they got engaged and we wanted the wedding to be a happy day for them. It was quite awkward at first but we all made an effort and the day went off smoothly.

Mike and I had been trying for a baby for almost two years when I fell pregnant. We were so happy – until Laura found out, that is. I think that she wanted to be 'first' in the family and her hostility towards me escalated. When my daughter was born she was very ill and I spent all my time next to her cot in the hospital fearing that she was going to die. Eddie came to visit us there, meet his niece and try to support us through such a terrible time, but Laura didn't come with him. She was pregnant by then and the reason given was that it would be too upsetting for her to see a baby in the intensive care ward. A few weeks later, we were still there. I remember that I'd been up all night with my daughter when I suddenly saw Laura appear in the corridor outside. I couldn't believe it! I thought she'd finally come to see her niece whose life was still in the balance. When I rushed out to see her she told me that she'd only come in for an appointment with her obstetrician.

Thankfully, my baby was well enough to go home after a while. When she was about seven months old we had a party for her and the whole family was invited. Laura turned up in such bad grace, complained about everything and eventually left in a huff. Eddie was embarrassed and angry with her, but I realised then that even though the 'getting there first' competition was over, there were years of competition ahead for all of us, including my innocent baby.

I'd like to be able to tell you that I was wrong. We've both had second children and she has had a third, but the comparisons just go on and on – about everything, from birth weight and the arrival of teeth to walking and talking. The children are all at nearby schools now and, when left to their own devices, they get on really well. My nephews come for tea with us but the invitation is seldom reciprocated. We have stopped attending the big family

Christmas and Mike and I try to protect the children from the fallout. If she had been a friend I'd have cut the ties a long time ago, but the problem with family is that you're stuck with them.

It's very difficult to understand sometimes where the sheer force of competitiveness comes from. What is obvious is its power to undermine and hurt. I asked many mothers how competitive they found motherhood and received a variety of interesting replies:

Poppy (35):

Competitive? Oh yes, definitely! Part of the reason I'm no good at mother-toddler meetings is because I can't stand the whole 'Oooh, little Johnny was walking at seven months, isn't she walking/talking/clean/playing football/ cooking a roast dinner yet?' malarkey. It drives me mad! It's all about whose baby is cuter, smarter and funnier and there's only so much of that I can tolerate. I tend to just stand back and let them get on with it. Gemma is only a year old. I have at *least* another 18 years to have this (or other similar) conversations, I've no intention of starting now. But when I do it'll hopefully be 'Gemma was accepted into Oxford *and* Cambridge University and she's having a heck of a time trying to figure out which one to go to'!

Sandra (30):

I think there can be a little competition, but perhaps more anxiety when your child doesn't seem to be doing the same things as those around you. It can make you panic that there's something wrong. But in the end you have to think – Well, they all get there in the end, so why worry?

Laura (29):

I think parenting can be very competitive if you let it. I look at people in Mothercare sometimes buying the 'latest' designer buggy or the four-poster crib and I think, who are you buying it for – you or your child? At the end of the day the child will be just as happy in economy class! Almost everything I have acquired since I became pregnant with my first child has been hand-me-downs from friends or secondhand. It is also competitive as far as milestones go. I just tend to ignore comments on what other children can do, say, draw or recite. Who cares – they all do their own thing in the end. As long as I feel I am doing the best I possibly can for my child's benefit (giving him a healthy diet, a good routine, and learning opportunities), then I don't really care what the rest of the world does.

Felicia (30):

I have not lost any friends since becoming a parent but I find it harder to maintain those friendships. Motherhood is very competitive and I have fallen victim to this as I am quite a competitive person. I can't help but judge other people's decisions if they are close to me and I am surprised by those decisions. My sister-in-law recently returned to work which, although I tried to support, I have found difficult to understand. I think this is a really negative aspect of being a mum. I have found that you are expected to be perfect – the perfect mother, the perfect career woman, look perfect and stay in shape, have perfect friendships, a perfect marriage. I feel a pressure from the media. My local newspaper is forever publishing negative articles on the pressures mothers face, implying women are responsible for a generation of overweight children with severe behavioural issues. Or that they are 'hothousing' their children when they are simply trying to do the best they can for their families.

Linda (32):

I haven't found motherhood competitive and I think it's really sad that some people do. It seems to me that it takes away all the good bits of parenting as you become so blinkered that you don't see what your child actually has achieved.

Maura (32):

Whenever you go anywhere baby-related (coffee mornings, baby swimming, etc.) everyone is talking about how much their child eats, how many teeth they have, how long they have been sleeping through the night, etc. They always start by asking you a question and then, when you answer, they say that their child has more teeth/eats more/sleeps longer/behaves better than yours! I'm not really interested, to be honest. As long as my daughter is happy and healthy

and roughly developing at a normal rate that's fine by me.

It told me something during the writing of this book that I didn't find one single woman who said that she actually enjoyed the competition between other mothers or that she took genuine pride in having a child who could do everything first and better than his contemporaries. Every woman interviewed felt that competition was sad, silly, negative or even downright dangerous.

How far does competitive motherhood have to go before we stop and look at what society is doing to mothers? The UK nursery market is now worth more than £3 billion. It is funded primarily by self-paying, private individuals. There is a distinct type of wealthy family, usually living in a big city and fearful for their children's success, that is pouring billions of pounds into creating what is known as an 'Alpha Child'.

The *Observer* reported in April 2005 that parents of pre-nursery-age children worry that the failure to get their child into the best nursery will set in motion a domino effect that will eventually shut their children out of the best universities. The Alpha Baby at one of these top-flight nurseries is under three years of age and is offered French, Japanese, music, painting and yoga as well as the usual activities. Swaddled in designer gear, he might know some Latin and be able to recognise Roman numerals as well as the usual numbers. For this privilege his parents are probably paying nigh on £200 a week. In some areas the nurseries that offer such hothousing are creating a stark contrast with the more common type of nursery which is less structured and more about providing space and fun for pre-schoolers to discover things for themselves. If these latter nurseries are losing customers it is not because the children are not thriving there but because increasingly competitive parents are panicking that their three-year-old hasn't been introduced to Latin like their friends' child at the nursery up the road.

I personally feel that this is very sad. I've looked after so many babies that I could make comparisons until the cows come home. But it's something I never get involved with. I try to keep parenting natural in the early years. There's plenty of time for pushing them further down the line if a parent feels they need it. My mother used to say, 'Georgie, you shouldn't be reaching for the stars so much that you miss the daisies at your feet.' I like to see mothers as stress-free as possible because most of them have got enough on their plate already without worrying about what their friend's neighbour's cousin's baby is doing. I have noticed that the mums in the country who spend a lot of time outside with their children, letting them run around and get dirty, seem less stressed than the city mums where competition is on every street corner. I can't understand why women put themselves and each other through it. I was talking to a mother the other day and she was so excited because her daughter could make the 'baby sign' for dog. She got a puzzled look from me because I was thinking that she'd be able to say the word in a few months' time. I wouldn't have said that to her of course because I believe in each to his own, but I truly hope her pleasure at this advance outweighed the stress of getting there.

In the past years the Internet has drawn us into a huge maelstrom. Women are at home a lot of the time with their babies, especially in the first few months. Many don't live in a community, with friends popping in for tea every half-hour, so, quite naturally, they go on to the many excellent parenting websites and chat to each other. When I was setting up www.contentedbaby.com the community aspect of it was crucial to me. Along with all the information, expert features and answers to questions, I wanted to provide a forum where mothers all over the world could come together and provide each other with friendship and support. I would look at the message board on other childcare sites and find that a handful of women were causing a riot, at each other's throats about every aspect of parenting, even the most bizarre. I went on to a site recently (not my own, I might add) and found that a woman had posted a question about oral sex, wondering if swallowing semen could make you pregnant. She received 150 replies. I confess to being baffled when I see 10 postings from one woman in the same morning. I wonder who's looking after the baby! Every aspect of parenting is mauled over on some chatroom websites and full-blown virtual catfights take place daily.

I wanted to create www.contentedbaby.com for followers of my routines. It was to be a safe haven for them; somewhere they knew they could come to talk to like-minded women. The site is just over a year old as this book goes to press. When I look at it I am overwhelmed by the hundreds of messages of support my mothers send to each other every month. Not once have I seen mothers criticising each other on my website and it makes me proud and happy.

Some of the biggest arguments on other websites and in the media seem to be about whether you are 'doing Gina Ford' or not. It provokes horrendous rows. It saddens me deeply that I seem to have inadvertently created a war among mothers. I wrote my books, in all innocence, for the sort of women who wanted routines for their babies. I never imagined what would come of it.

I certainly did not intend to create this uproar. And most assuredly I never wanted to create divides between women. I assumed that if a mother didn't want to follow my routines then she would ignore them and do her own thing. When mothers I work with phone me, upset because they have encountered an aggressive mother from the AGFB (the Anti Gina Ford Brigade, as my team call it), they sometimes ask me how I cope. I tell them that I just ignore it and carry on with my work. I am here to give advice to the women who *want* to make structure work for them. If they don't want to use it, it's fine by me. If a woman wants to feed on demand or sleep with her baby, I do not, ever, think that she is a bad mother or that she is damaging her child. Its not about what I think: it's about what *you* want and *you* think. We live in a democracy.

The power of women has slowed down in the last 20 years, since those heady days of feminism when so much was achieved to improve the lives of women. Sometimes I think we've lost the plot a bit. We are doing ourselves a huge disservice by fighting each other and fighting men. We have stopped making life better for women. I feel that many women are wasting their energies fighting among themselves about the little things, like teat sizes and breast pads, and so don't have the energy to focus on the wider aspects of mothering. If women are to have it all, as we are told and want, we should be aiming at teaching women as much as possible about the different choices available to them in mothering. Then they can choose whichever style of parenting they feel suits them best. Each mother has the right to make her own choices. I don't teach women about emotions. I believe in empowering women to live their lives, as mothers – and as people in their own right.

It seems the key to competitiveness lies in the insecurity that goes so naturally, in some degree, with motherhood for many women. Of course the mums at playgroup are going to ask how soon each other's children learned to walk, talk, etc. It's the main currency of conversation between mothers and it can be a great bonding experience – or it can leave women feeling inadequate, guilty and anxious. The media and the world at large bombard mothers with negative messages. Mothers cannot please everyone and they shouldn't even try. There are many, many mothers out there wondering whether they are 'good' or 'bad' and suffering untold stress and anxiety.

My message to all mothers at the end of this chapter is *not* to make war on each other, but to be tolerant of each other and honest with each other. I concur entirely with family seminar host and author, Rob Parsons, who writes in *The Sixty Minute Mother*: 'From what they tell me, most mothers don't want clever answers, and they certainly don't want clever answers from those who pretend they've got it all sorted. What they want most of all is for another mother to whisper to them, "This isn't just you – we've all been there, done it and worn the T-shirt."' He goes on to remind his readers that there are two really important words that mothers need to say to one another: ME TOO.

Chapter 6

❈

Breast

is

Best

❈

My mother couldn't help getting involved in my work. Like most of us, she was interested in what happened in other people's lives, and she had a sympathy and understanding of mothers and the awful situations they went through. Still, there were times when I could have done without her understanding and sympathising quite so much. Like the time my phone rang, and my mother was on the other end, telling me she'd just been talking to Penny, one of my clients.

'That poor girl,' said my mother. 'She's going through hell, breast-feeding. It's just not working. Angus is screaming his head off night and day. She's feeding him every two hours, and he's eleven weeks old. Her nipples are practically falling off, she's stressed, exhausted and worried out of her mind. I've never heard a woman in such a state. But don't worry, I helped her out.'

'What did you say, Mum?' I asked anxiously.

'It's fine,' she replied blithely. 'I told her to just go out, get some Cow & Gate, and feed that baby some formula. It's obvious the poor child is starving.'

I nearly dropped the phone in horror. 'You can't do that!' I cried. 'First off, you know I support breast-feeding for babies, and second, what if it gets out that Gina Ford is saying just go out and get some formula? The National Childbirth Trust will send out death squads! I'll be lynched in the street!'

'Oh, Gina, calm down. What does it matter? The important thing is, the child is starving and the mother is in a terrible state. It's the baby we need to think of, and if help is at hand, she ought to use it.'

In one stroke, my mother flagged up the simple part of the complex arguments surrounding feeding our babies.

Breast-feeding is wonderful. It is the natural way to feed our babies. Breast milk is the best food for babies – but thank goodness we've got other, healthy ways to keep our children alive and flourishing when breast-feeding doesn't work.

My mother breast-fed me for two days before her milk supply gave out and she moved on to formula feeding. She was not worried about this because she came from a generation of post-war mothers who believed that formula was at least as good as breast milk, if not better. Unlike today, there was a great deal of trust in manufactured products that promised they were an improvement on what nature could offer. Who can blame these women? Not only could this generation see all around them the improvements that science, technology and medicine were bringing to their world, but they had recent memories of malnourished, starving infants and of children who died when breast-feeding failed or was not possible. Before the advent of a viable alternative to breast milk and, just as importantly, a reliable and clean way to feed it to a baby, hand feeding, as it was known, was a virtual death sentence. Because the constituents of breast milk were not understood, attempts to replicate it were disastrous. Extraordinary mixtures were recommended, but most often flour and milk or water were mixed together to create 'pap'; sugar water and animal milk were also used but survival on these was, not surprisingly, low. In her book *Yesterday's Babies*, Diana Dick reported that 'the Dublin Foundling Hospital, which hand fed over 10,000 infants in the twenty-one years between 1775 and 1796, had only forty-five survivors – a staggering 99.6% mortality rate!'

It wasn't until the early years of the twentieth century, when scientists were able to analyse breast milk and re-create it as closely as possible, and when the use of indiarubber was applied to create sterile teats, that children who couldn't be breast-fed had the chance of safe nourishment. One doctor quoted in *The Baby Book* of 1908, published by Glaxo, writes of a baby of three months suffering from diarrhoea and vomiting. He has tried to feed it with 'beef juice, albumen water, whey and cream, patented food, cow's milk, water etc, but to no avail' but after trying Glaxo's formula, he declares that 'it saved the baby's life' – and it almost certainly did.

It's no wonder that my mother and her generation saw formula milk as a miracle and that they took to bottle-feeding with a gusto that would shock today's mothers. It wasn't just that formula was regarded as superior nourishment; a lot of women saw breast-feeding as animalistic and were turned off by the whole idea. For them, bottle-feeding was the more civilised route. In fact, my mother was inordinately proud of the fact that I was a Cow & Gate baby, and not fed on National Health milk like my cousins.

These attitudes may be difficult to understand now. Our society is completely transformed and, thank goodness, the levels of poverty that killed so many children are almost unknown. Mothers are, on the whole, better nourished and less overworked, and more capable of feeding their children themselves, especially as most don't have six, seven or more children. We no longer see formula milk as a miracle able to nourish deprived infants better than their mother. Instead, we are much more aware that breast milk is by far the best food for a baby, with health benefits to both child and mother, and the modern mission is to help and encourage as many mothers as possible to breast-feed.

In Britain, breast-feeding rates are extremely low compared to the rest of Europe and the developed world. Sixty-nine per cent of mothers begin breast-feeding immediately their baby is born but that drops to 52 per cent after two weeks and to 42 per cent at six weeks. Only 21 per cent of babies are still breast-fed at six months. In the UK, government guidelines recommend exclusive breast milk until babies reach six months of age. If we accept that in an ideal world all mothers, barring those physically incapable, would breast-feed their babies for six months, then there is clearly a long way to go.

So why don't more women breast-feed? The reasons are varied. In the course of my career I have spoken to thousands of women with new babies as they take on the task of feeding. I may never have breast-fed a baby myself but I know virtually everything about cracked nipples, leaky boobs, husbands who feel they've lost their wives sexually, the frustrations and the joys of breast-feeding. Some women don't breast-feed because their mothers did not and they don't see any reason to change. Many more start out with the best of intentions, but lack of advice and support when they find it more difficult than they had expected overturns their efforts. The feelings of self-doubt, guilt and misery that go hand in hand with this are deep-rooted and profound ones in modern society. Women suffer over this single issue of baby care more than any other.

Many professionals feel that the problems start in the earliest days in hospital, and certainly I always felt that the old rigid feeding-every-four-hours schedule was simply not enough for a breast-feeding mother, which is why I developed my own routines. These days, some people feel that over-stretched midwives are too quick to give a bottle to a hungry newborn because they don't have the time to sit down and teach a mother what to do.

The truth is that breast-feeding usually has to be learned, unless you are one of those lucky women whose baby pops out and then starts gobbling on the breast like a natural.

Sindy (35) works in the film industry. She had no problems at all breast-feeding either of her daughters.

When I was pregnant for the first time, I was 100 per cent sure I would breast-feed. I felt it was the ultimate function of my breasts but also that it was easy and cheap, as well as the best nutrition possible for my baby. The fact that it would help me get my figure back was on the list of appealing factors too! My mum breast-fed my brother and me for almost a year and she was very positive about it while I was expecting. After a relatively easy birth I put

Olivia straight to the breast. I remember that it was much more painful than I'd thought it would be. On day three the midwife came to see me and I told her how painful I was finding it. She told me I wasn't positioning Olivia correctly, then she literally grabbed my entire breast and shoved it into the baby's mouth. She told me it was called breast-feeding not nipple-feeding. She was absolutely right and it quickly got easier with some practice from both of us. My husband was very supportive too.

Olivia was a champion breast-feeder and would always feed for about an hour. I was lucky that I always seemed to have plenty of milk and I never had mastitis or any other problems. I could never remember which side was the next one to feed from and I used to lie on the floor to see which breast was fuller. I devised elaborate ways of remembering which was next by tying ribbons to my bra straps, but then I couldn't remember whether I'd changed it over after the last feed or not. That's the jelly brain of early motherhood, I suppose.

I found it very bonding and I loved that I could always comfort her when she was crying. I was very reluctant to give up breast-feeding. They were my 'big guns' which would always make her happy. When she was eleven months old, though, I felt it had gone past feeding and she was using it as comfort alone. I also began to want my body back for myself by then. I felt a bit criticised by other people as well, for feeding beyond nine months. This child had a full set of teeth and I felt other people thought she was too big for the breast. I didn't give in to that pressure, but her dependence worried me. She would never take a bottle from me or anyone so I weaned her straight on to a cup. After a few tough days we both adjusted, but I felt very emotional about it, as if a bond between us had been broken. But as soon as my breasts returned to normal I felt fine and I'll always be happy I got her off to such a great start.

Second time around it was more functional and less emotional. I can certainly remember the first experience of breast-feeding better than the second. Amy was much less into the breast than her sister. Her feeds were shorter. I felt more confident that she would settle without being breast-fed to sleep. It was a lot less peaceful, as Olivia always seemed to be making mayhem around the house while I was trying to feed. I fed for six months but stopped for work commitments. Weaning was very easy and straight-forward. I didn't feel the bonding so much with Amy but ironically I now feel closer to her than Olivia so I know that nothing was lost in terms of closeness because of the length of time they were breast-fed. My mum's encouragement and support while I was feeding both girls and also when I wanted to stop was incredibly important to me.

Sindy is lucky that breast-feeding was easy for her and was a successful and happy experience. She had great support from her own mother. Mothers who do find it easy to breast-feed can become very intense about its benefits. Some want to go on for as long as possible and are completely convinced of its benefits not just for newborns but for toddlers.

Camilla (41) has breast-fed all her children for as long as they wanted. She has two sons as well as a daughter, aged two, who is still on the breast.

I can't think of anything more natural than a mother feeding her children. I feel really strongly about it. I threw myself into it when my first son was born and I'm still doing it now. I have the complete support of my husband and most of my friends know how I feel about breast-feeding. I do feed in public if I have to and I don't always like the looks people give me. But I know I am doing the right thing for my children and that keeps me determined not to cave in to pressure from others. Breast milk is the perfect food and can provide wonderful nutrition and lifelong health benefits through its antibodies and other positive effects, things we're just learning about. For instance, not only are the children less likely to suffer from allergies and colds, they'll also be more protected against heart disease, cancer, diabetes and obesity. There's also protection for me because a breast-feeding mother is less likely to get breast or uterine cancer in the future. It's just wonderful for all of us.

The boys both fed until they were about three. I let them take the lead to stop and the day came when each one stopped asking for 'boobie'. My eldest son stopped but briefly wanted to join in when he saw his baby brother feeding. I didn't feel I could tell him no, but he wasn't interested for long. I feel that feeding them whenever they have wanted to be close to me has given them both great inner confidence and strength. Whenever they've been stressed or unhappy, a quick quiet breast-feed has helped them enormously. I also get the benefit because it releases oxytocin, which is a happy hormone – it relaxes you and makes you feel better.

There is a downside because I've been breast-feeding almost continuously for seven years and sometimes I feel that my boobs don't belong to me any more. After days and nights of getting them out for the children, my husband comes at the bottom of the list. It's hard on our sex life but this stage of our lives will be over for ever soon and we both feel strongly that the children have had the best possible start to life.

Most mothers don't consider breast-feeding after one year, and many aim to breast-feed for six months. Some would consider Camilla's reluctance to let a bottle near their child as going a bit too far, and are happy to offer expressed breast milk in bottles from the early days, or to supplement their feeding with formula feeds.

Mothers who find it relatively easy to breast-feed are the lucky ones. Sometimes it is hard for those who've found it a breeze to understand the difficulty other women can experience. Clare Byam-Cook, one of the UK's leading breast-feeding counsellors who has helped thousands of mothers in her career and who is a regular contributor to my website, says, 'I see women who on day four have got enough milk to feed five babies, and they just can't understand why anyone would give a bottle. They don't realise that banging on to a failed breast-feeder does no good at all. It's like having a go at a woman who's just had a third miscarriage and saying "You should really have a baby, it's wonderful". But just because you've got all the right bits doesn't mean it's going to work – I mean, if you have eyes, it doesn't mean you're going to have perfect vision. I certainly think that every woman should try and breast-feed – I don't like people saying "Oh, it doesn't appeal to me" – but if you try and it just isn't working, then there's a time to say, that's enough.'

Many women feel that they were simply unprepared for how difficult breast-feeding would be. The general understanding is that it's entirely natural and as easy as falling off a log, and even women who've attended antenatal classes and workshops can be left in the dark about what it really entails.

Maria (31), told me about her own experience:

I thought it was your own decision whether you chose breast or bottle feed, and you might bottle-feed because you might not like the feeling of breast-feeding or something – I never thought you might not have the choice.

I went to antenatal classes but mostly they focused on the birth and the breast-feeding bit was fairly quick – it was fifteen minutes with a doll, and that was it. There was a picture of how to latch a baby on, so I thought it must be simple. You just hold it in your arms and plonk it on your breast. Friends had said breast-feeding was hard but I thought that was to do with cracked nipples, so that was all I knew beforehand. To be honest, I don't think I know an awful lot more now.

I fed Clive the first time in hospital and I'd had a lot of after-pain following the birth, so I had to do it lying on my side in bed. The people there were very nice, but they weren't really prepared to teach me to breast-feed, it was almost as though that wasn't their job. The midwife latched him on for me and said, 'Take a big chunk of breast in your hand and get the baby to bite on all of it, not just the nipple.' That was all I was told. And as I always fed lying on my side, I thought it was fine that they latched him on and went away. He fed and it seemed okay.

Then I went home. I still did mostly lie down to feed and after a few days I sat up and started doing it that way. It seemed all right to start with. The midwife came twice and said it was fine – everyone who talked to me was lovely and I had no concept that they might not be giving me the information I'd need. Then my milk came in – and I never knew that was going to happen! I had no idea it would be so painful and I'd have two great cauliflowers on the front of my chest. I thought, 'What the hell is happening?' and got my books out and that helped, because I learned to express and take hot baths and so on, to relieve it. But the books still said the same old thing about how to latch the baby on – and it just didn't seem the best way. Even now, I get so angry when I see other people breast-feeding and they're obviously doing it differently from the way I was told.

For the first six weeks, it was quite a normal experience and he seemed to feed quite well. I even remember I liked getting up at 3am and feeding the baby, because I felt a real glow of motherhood. He regained his birth weight and we got into more of a routine with his feeding. At my six-week check, I said, 'Breast-feeding is going great, I think I've got it'; then about two days later, it all suddenly went wrong. Feeds got quickly more unsettled and Clive would be hungry, go on the breast, feed very well for one to two minutes and then he'd suddenly scream and pull away in absolute fury. I'd try and burp him and comfort him, and he'd carry on crying. I knew he was still hungry and I'd try and put him back on. He'd be pleased, then he'd suck, I could hear him swallow and then, when it hit his stomach, I'd hear a gurgle and he'd start screaming. He'd be inconsolable. The pain would subside, then he'd be hungry and I couldn't solve the problem because he was either hungry or in pain . . . this would take an hour and a half.

Between six and 10 weeks, I saw the health visitor. I was worried about the seal around his mouth and that he was maybe swallowing air. The health visitor said everything was fine. She didn't have a suitable chair in her room so she wasn't able to see how I really fed him and I was totally uncomfortable on the footstool in her room. When I think about it, it wasn't helpful at all.

A week later, I told her it was a nightmare and she came over to watch me feed in my own environment. He did the usual thing and pulled off, screaming. She told me to stop after 40 minutes but I knew he was still hungry. Her comments were: 'He's latching on fine, he's sucking, you've got milk – it's fine. Be positive about each feed and it will settle down.' I gave up on the health visitor after that.

I had a doctor's appointment for something else, and brought up the problem. I said I was considering expressing because I'd tried a bottle and it hadn't seemed so bad. The doctor was quite positive about it, whereas the health visitor had not been. But after ten weeks, I said, 'I'm not doing this any more.' I'd been crying at every feed, and I could see the baby was very unhappy and it wasn't working. I expressed three times a day and went on to some formula feeds, but it was still happening, even with the bottle. He'd pull away and get gurgly. Then my supply diminished so I went on to formula but he was still screaming. I tried different, thicker formulas meant for babies who find it difficult to digest milk. It was awful. Clive would cry when he saw the bottle, and he farted all night as well.

The doctor said, 'Try Infant Gaviscon – it's meant for babies with reflux but it might help his digestion.' It seemed to help but really, the only thing that settled him was when I put him into a routine of feeding plus the Gaviscon – and I've since been told I may have been over-feeding him in my anxiety – and then started weaning him.

If I have another baby, I'm nervous about breast-feeding. I wanted to breast-feed, I really did but I couldn't and it was such a lonely, horrible experience. I couldn't go out because of Clive's screaming and it made me think I was a bad mother. I found it hard to give up breast-feeding; it was very difficult because I wanted to keep going and wanted to succeed. When I realised it wasn't the best thing for Clive, I knew I had to stop – he was so unhappy.

The most damaging bit was the loneliness that led to depression. I left a message on the NCT breast-feeding helpline but no one called back and I got a letter a month later asking if I wanted to join. I didn't know how to find a counsellor and no one suggested it. The health visitor thought she knew enough. Clive's first four months were a time of grief for me, rather than a time of happiness.

I suspect that Clive had reflux and my heart goes out to someone who had this difficult experience. Maria is by no means the only one. The trouble is that not enough midwives and health visitors are given full training as breast-feeding specialists, and they simply don't know how to help. But it is the luck of the draw – where you live will influence the kind of help you have. It's not always easy to ask for help, either. As Caroline (32) told me:

> I had chronic eczema as a child and still suffer quite badly at times. It was purely for that reason I wanted to breast-feed Sara and give her a chance of not getting that or the asthma that often accompanies it. I also felt a bit bullied into it by my community midwife and doctors giving me the 'breast is best' speech at every opportunity. But the truth is that I hated every second of it. I am quite short, with a short torso, and Sara was very long which meant that we just couldn't get comfy. As a result I stopped after six weeks. I had lots of support but I felt awkward about asking and I'm sure that it could have helped. I guess support differs from area to area. My sister's support network was fantastic and she utilised it fully. I felt awkward about it.

Some hospitals have wonderful breast-feeding support systems, and are doing their best to persuade every mother to breast-feed for as long as she can, certainly in the earliest days, to give their babies the best possible start. There are also organisations like La Leche League, the National Childbirth Trust and www.thewaynatureintended.org who promote and support breast-feeding and help mothers in difficulty. The key, though, is to understand that every woman is different. While support for breast-feeding is very important and necessary, particularly in deprived areas where breast-feeding rates are extremely low, it can be taken to extremes.

Clare Byam-Cook told me:

There are hospitals in London where, because of lack of proper teaching, mothers are being sent home unable to feed. The babies are coming back, ill and seriously dehydrated. Just because a baby's sucking at the breast, he may not be getting milk. If the baby can't latch on in the hospital, why on earth will he suddenly start doing it when they get home? I was so angry about this, I wrote to a consultant paediatrician at one of the big hospitals, who told me that he shared my concerns. He said, 'I totally agree that we are readmitting an unacceptable number of dehydrated babies, caused by wrong and inappropriate advice by the midwives. But what can we do?' Another paediatrician said that he'd heard their hospital breast-feeding counsellor say that she would rather see every baby readmitted to the hospital and put on a drip than given a bottle. This seems to me to be the kind of attitude that will frighten mothers rather than reassure them.

For mothers who enjoy breast-feeding their first babies, things often prove more difficult second or third time around when there is a demanding toddler to take into account. Debbie (34) told me:

I loved breast-feeding my first son although it took us both a while to get the hang of it. The sleepy closeness of feeding is like nothing else. I spent an hour or so, several times a day, sitting quietly with Peter. I read a book or watched the sort of trashy daytime television I had never seen during my working life. As long as I remembered my large glass of water and the muslin cloth, I could sit for a long time and nurse him peacefully. I didn't even mind the night feeds as it felt like such a special, close time. We kept going for about six months until an infection meant I had to stop. I was sad about this, but mainly glad to have had such a wonderful experience.

When Michael was born two years later my main worries at first were for Peter. I wanted to involve him with the baby and to reassure him how much he was loved. I feared that he would be jealous of my time feeding. It was fine sometimes and I made sure Peter had a video to watch or a book we could read together while I fed the baby. I had to be really organised with getting him a drink or snack beforehand to avoid interruptions. But it was so difficult at other times. I remember building a train track with one hand while holding the baby on to the breast with my other hand. I only had those peaceful quiet feeds during the night and first thing in the morning. Once, I was feeding quietly inside when there were screams from the garden. Peter had gone outside on his own and ridden his toy car down a slope. I wrenched the baby off the breast, left him yelling on his mat and flew outside to find a snotty toddler in a pile of leaves.

My milk supply was never the same second time round and by seven weeks I was so exhausted from looking after both the boys that I could barely meet Michael's feeding needs. An infection meant I needed antibiotics and had to stop and, while I was relieved that other people could now help and that I wouldn't have to cope with two lots of very urgent demands, I still feel very sad that I never had that special time with my second child.

It's at times such as Debbie describes that another pair of hands can make all the difference. If Debbie had had more childcare for her first son, or a relative or neighbour nearby to take Peter out for the afternoon now and again, she might have been able to feed her baby herself for longer. As it was, she was on her own without any support.

A nightmare story came to me via my website and my heart ached for first-time mum, Annie (aged 31). Her story illustrates the isolation that many mothers experience, even when health professionals are consulted. She had always assumed that she would breast-feed and, like many women, had attended a breast-feeding instruction evening during her pregnancy. She felt very positive about it.

As soon as Andrew was born he was put to my breast and started to suck. The midwives in the hospital were really helpful and showed me the correct way to position him, and he seemed to be doing just fine. We went home when Andrew was two days old and the community midwife signed us off. Andrew's weight gain was below average – he had gained 4 ounces after two weeks, but she reassured me that it sometimes takes breast-fed babies a while to regain their birth weight and start putting on weight properly.

My health visitor first came to see us when Andrew was

three weeks old, and by then he had gained only another 4 ounces and I was starting to worry. He didn't seem very happy, cried a lot, and would only sleep on the breast or lying on my husband's tummy. We were starting to feel a bit desperate for sleep. She watched us breast-feed and said that we looked like we were doing it correctly. I was concerned that I had never felt a let-down reflex or heard him swallowing and that he spent so much time on the breast, but I was told that this was all quite normal.

But Andrew cried and cried. He was calm when on the breast, but then he would quickly fall asleep only to wake screaming the moment I laid him on his bed. As I pushed my wailing infant round the park in his pram, praying that he would fall asleep long enough for me to drink a cup of tea when we got home, there were times I honestly wished he'd never been born. I was so tired I could hardly speak, Andrew's weight gain was seriously low (about 2–3 ounces a week) and still the health professionals I saw insisted that there was nothing wrong. I even saw an NCT breast-feeding counsellor every week at a parentcraft class we attended, but while she was extremely supportive and positive, she couldn't see anything wrong.

You must be wondering why I didn't just give Andrew a bottle of formula and it sounds so stupid, but I honestly didn't realise that his problem was hunger. He was always feeding, filled lots of nappies and looked like he was doing it right. Everyone told me Andrew was doing fine. At the 10-week check our GP expressed concerns about his weight and said that ordinarily she would recommend I supplement the breast-feeding with formula milk, but because of

Andrew's eczema and my worries about allergies she would review the situation a fortnight later. My health visitor had confirmed that I was developing postnatal depression by this point but still there was no suggestion from anyone that we had a feeding problem.

I went to the baby clinic then, hoping that someone would be able to advise me, but the health visitor just frightened me even more by reminding me of the seriousness of the situation. She told me that I must put Andrew to the breast every two hours. I sobbed all the way home and spent the rest of the day and the whole of the following night trying to feed Andrew. The eczema on his cheeks was so inflamed by being pressed up against my arm that it was cracked and oozing and the fabric of my clothes was sticking to him. I rang the GP's surgery the next morning in tears and managed to get a consultant paediatrician to see us that same day.

The consultant examined Andrew, said that he 'could see no evidence of anything seriously wrong with him' and prescribed soya formula, and antibiotics and ointments for his skin. My husband gave Andrew his first bottle when we got home and for the first time in his 13 weeks of life Andrew fell asleep peacefully. It was like flipping a switch – we went from having a screaming, nightmare baby to the most contented, happy baby you could ever meet. Suddenly everything was wonderful. My depression lifted, and I fell head over heels in love with my son. I stopped breast-feeding immediately: how could I carry on after all we'd been through?

I know the responsibility for feeding my baby was

ultimately mine and that I was stupid enough to put his health at risk, but I do feel angry that we were let down by the health professionals. Surely someone should have told me what was blatantly obvious – my baby was hungry. I will never stop feeling ashamed and guilty for continuing with breast-feeding as long as I did, but all I ever wanted was what was right for my baby, and depressed, exhausted first-time mothers don't always make good decisions.

The desperate sense of failure and panic when your breast-fed baby is screaming is overwhelming in Annie's story. Not surprisingly, she begins to develop postnatal depression. The most powerful part of her story is her relief when her baby's hunger is finally satiated by a bottle of formula after 13 weeks of struggle, misery and exhaustion.

Just as our health professionals and modern society at large seem to be sending women the message that breast-feeding makes you a good mother, so it's implied that if you bottle-feed you are a bad mother. In 2005 Professor Frank Furedi and Dr Ellie Lee of the University of Kent published a vitally important study on the political aspects of feeding a baby. They set out to investigate the effects for women of a cultural and social context in which the message that 'breast is best' is strongly promoted. Their conclusions were startling. They found that 50 per cent of women felt under pressure to breast-feed. Forty-four per cent felt that women who didn't were made to feel guilty. The fact that using formula makes many women feel like failures creates divisions between women. They found women who had hidden their bottles in their bags at mums' meetings and ones who had felt ostracised by the breast-feeders for feeding their baby formula milk. It also creates a trust gap between health professionals and the very people they are trying to support and help, as women lie about their feeding methods to avoid criticism or pressure.

Furedi and Lee strongly concluded that breast-feeding has become a highly moral issue and that the disapproval felt by women who don't breast-feed is dangerous. The report recommends that formula feeding be depoliticised and viewed as a routine part of baby care rather than a moral issue. Women need to be informed about the benefits of breast-feeding but without the negativity attached to using formula.

In my conversations with feeding mothers, and in the interviews conducted for this book, I have come across few who feel no sense of pressure or guilt about how they feed their babies. One of the exceptions was Glenda (44). She combined formula and breast-feeding with success and, crucially, with complete confidence:

Before my first child was born, I had already decided to breast-feed, believing it was good for both baby and mother, although I don't remember reading much about the practical aspects – I just thought, rather naively, that it would be a natural and instinctive process. My first child, Richard, was born three weeks early weighing 5 pounds 15 ounces. I recall the first few days after the birth being very difficult, coping with the after-effects of a C-section and a general anaesthetic plus a baby who was hungry but, because of his size, unable to latch on or feed easily. In the beginning I had to call a midwife to assist me every time I needed to feed and I found this extremely frustrating. But after four days both Richard and I at last worked out what to do!

Breast-feeding then became a relatively stress-free and enjoyable part of our day. During the first few weeks I was feeding on demand with the help of formula. Each morning I would make up two 4-ounce bottles and use them at varying times through the day. Sometimes towards the end of the day when I was feeling tired and Richard was unsettled, my husband would give him a bottle, which was the perfect solution for everyone: my husband got a chance to bond with his son, Richard got a full feed when my supply seemed inadequate and I got a welcome break. Giving formula late in the evening also seemed to help him to settle for the first few hours of the night.

I generally used one bottle at night and the other when my milk supply felt low, or when it was simply more convenient to bottle-feed. Despite his low birth weight, Richard gained up to 13 ounces a week with this approach, and rapidly hit the 98th centile for height and 75th centile for weight. This feeding pattern continued for almost six months, and the bottles of formula increased in time to 8-ounce feeds. I decided to stop breast-feeding at six months, so I simply dropped one feed at a time and replaced it with a bottle. Once I moved on to formula exclusively at six months, I remember being more fastidious about daily milk intake, but when I was mixed feeding, I didn't concern myself too much with intake or minutes per breast; rather I kept an eye on his weight gain and this seemed to be fine.

I remember reading at the time that offering a combination of breast and bottle could have an adverse effect on milk supply, confuse the baby and lead many mothers to give up breast-feeding altogether. I was, however, confident that my method was working for Richard and me, so I paid little attention to the reservations of others and just stuck with it.

When Richard's sister Sylvie arrived she was two weeks late and weighed 10 pounds 3 ounces. Sylvie was ravenous from the beginning and was able to latch on immediately. Again I fed on demand, but as she was able to take a lot more milk at a single feed than smaller babies, she could easily go for four hours between feeds. When I brought her home from hospital, again I introduced mixed feeding, which, looking back, was essential for my well-being. Sylvie was such a hungry baby, particularly in the evenings; she would want to feed for literally hours until I was completely exhausted and empty. Again, the bottles were a saviour as they gave her the extra volume she needed to sleep. With a baby and toddler to look after, I found it convenient to give Sylvie a bottle at lunchtime too, as it was easier to give Richard his lunch at the same time. I breast-fed Sylvie for six months, again tailing off gradually towards the end.

The relaxed method I adopted worked very well for my family as it gave us a degree of flexibility while enabling me to continue breast-feeding for six months with each child. Without the help of the little bottles of formula in the fridge each day, I know that I would not have been able to maintain breast-feeding and would have given up much sooner.

Even if you support breast-feeding, as I do, there are then complicated issues about how to do it, and for how long. Part of the debate is the conflict between demand feeding and feeding on a routine. It's not going to surprise you to learn that I feel that demand feeding is not the best thing for mothers and babies. That simple statement has caused an enormous amount of outrage and debate, and the erroneous belief that I think babies should be allowed to go hungry. People who are anti-routine paint the picture of a piteous baby crying desperately for food while the stern mother stands by, looking at the clock and refusing to feed until it is the right time. This picture is a vivid one and also, I'm glad to say, entirely wrong. Nowhere in any of my books do I advocate leaving a hungry baby unfed. If a young baby is crying long before the times I recommend, then of course that baby must be fed. But I suggest that mothers look for the reasons that a baby needs feeding every one to two hours. If you move towards a routine as best you can, your baby will not go hungry provided he takes a full feed. I've evolved my routines over many years of looking after babies and they are based very carefully on the natural rhythms of a baby. In the past, breast-feeding could fail because the routine was based on strict four-hourly schedules. I've changed that in my own routines so that breast-feeding can succeed.

Babies must be fed, no matter what their schedule; it is the term 'demand feeding' that I'm opposed to. Feeding on demand – i.e. little and often, whenever the baby cries – can work for some people but it doesn't work for everyone and it is those people I'm trying to help. Picking up the baby to feed it every time it cries is not always the answer, and it doesn't encourage the mother to look for other reasons why their baby might be crying, such as over-tiredness or discomfort. The result so often is a mother desperately trying to feed a child who will not stop crying because something else entirely is the matter. A lot of very young babies are sleepy and don't always demand to be fed. If a baby sleeps a lot of the day it will be hard to establish successful breast-feeding, because the breasts are not getting enough stimulation to establish the sort of milk supply that will be needed for a good six months of feeding.

My routines arose from my observations of contented babies and what they wanted to do naturally, as well as what would help the mother. I see it as the best of both worlds – being able to breast-feed but also able to *cope* with breast-feeding. For a lot of mothers, being up ten times a night as well as feeding all day for months on end is too hard to face. I hope I can help those mothers to find some peace and continue breast-feeding when they might have given up. I also hope that those women who choose to use formula milk, for whatever reason, will not be consumed with guilt or be judged as bad mothers by the health professionals or by one another.

So many experiences of motherhood are kept secret because women feel guilt and shame about not being perfect. It's hard to hide your feeding choices from family and friends, but there are aspects of motherhood that are hidden by mothers anxious to appear 'in control' and, thus, a good mother. Feelings of guilt and shame can be very powerful. It makes me sad that so many women are experiencing the same things but are unable to talk about them to each other and find the comfort and reassurance that they need. For example, over and over I have heard how breast-feeding affects a mother's sex life. There is the same associated guilt and inevitable feelings of inadequacy.

Mary finished feeding her child at six months. Tiredness affected her sex life primarily, but as she told me, 'You really feel like a mother first and foremost while you are breast-feeding and not a sexual being. My breasts belonged to me and my baby and I hated my partner going anywhere near them.' Another story came from Felicity, who didn't enjoy breast-feeding at all. 'I have absolutely no feeling in my nipples now whatsoever, not one jot! Is it a mental thing, I wonder?' The majority of women I spoke to who had breast-fed said that either they or their partners were uncomfortable with breasts being part of their postnatal sex life. As Amanda (30) told me: 'It's hell on the sex life. You can't be a cow and feel sexy.'

What so many women openly report after having a baby is the exhaustion and shock of it, all mixed up together with the overwhelming love for the baby and frightening sense of responsibility. What you only find if you ask the right questions is that many women begin to lose a sense of them-selves in the all-consuming task of caring for their baby. One of the most crucial ways all humans define themselves is sexually. After a baby arrives the roles in a marriage are more clearly defined than ever before, especially if one of the parties is being a milk cow, as Amanda said. If the mother is feeding the baby and sleeping in another room from her husband, or the marital bed is now the family bed, the couple's sex life is unlikely to recover from the birth or to flourish as the months go by.

The lack of a sex life can underline this loss of self that many women feel. Making love on Saturday night with your husband might be all you got round to before but, hell, it's better than nothing and the stress that grows up if this aspect of a relationship suffers may add to the weight of resentment and guilt that so many women bear in the postnatal months. If you are already questioning whether you are a good mother you really don't want to add 'Am I good wife?' to the self-flagellation. Judging by the amount of stories I have been told during my research for this book, this is a far from unusual experience. And, while it might seem difficult to bring up the subject of sex during breast-feeding over the tea and HobNobs when you're with your new mums' group, you would not find yourselves alone by a long shot. It's perhaps not something the average breast-feeding counsellor will have a view on; here your best allies are women in the same situation.

❉

Chapter 7

Mothers
of
Men

❉

My mother's relationship with her mother-in-law was never going to be easy. My mother had married one of the adored sons of a matriarchal woman whose chief aim in life had been to put 'her boys' on pedestals and make sure they always remained there.

I was my parents' first and only child, and the story of my introduction to my paternal grandmother always makes me laugh. My arrival in the world had been a long and arduous experience for my mother. A 48-hour labour left her bruised and exhausted, and unlike many mothers today she had found it neither spiritual nor transcending! Two weeks after the birth, my mother was at home, still weak and confined to bed. Over in the cradle in the corner of her bedroom was this little black-haired baby, Georgina. Me. My grandmother arrived, bustling and busy, all of a flutter with the changes that had taken places in the family. She was armed with a box of chocolates and a bottle of lemonade. She gave a cursory glance at the new baby, and then, as my father walked into the room, her face lit up with pride and she handed him her offerings.

'These are for you, my son,' she announced. 'To keep your strength up.'

A treat for her precious son. And for my mother? Not a damn thing.

I laugh about it, but I felt sorry for my mother in just the same way I've felt sorry for a lot of the mothers I've worked with when they've had problems with thoughtless, insensitive mothers-in-law. Those who think the way they brought up their children is the only way to do it and insist on taking over. It used to astonish me that in the midst of this remarkable new family, a mother-in-law could appear, and fail to recognise that she was walking on proverbial eggshells. Yet I have also felt sorry for grandparents, denied the pleasure of being closely involved with their new grandchildren by too over-sensitive, over-protective daughters-in-law.

My grandmother was a very strong-minded, fearless woman, who had given birth to ten children and raised them in difficult financial circumstances. My grandfather was a pitman, as was my father and all of his brothers. The men in the family were typical of a certain type of chauvinistic, northern, working-class man of the time, and they were hugely in awe of my grandmother, who ran the family with a fierce determination and ferocious pride. She was an extraordinary woman – principled and tough. Into this family arrived my mother. A woman who was every bit as determined, but not one who was prepared to fit quietly into the place intended for her.

My grandmother would preside over the table, her large family gathered around her, pouring tea and putting the sugar in for them. This was a woman who doted on her boys, and expected both her daughters and the wives that would come into the family to do the same. For her sons nothing was too much trouble. She buttered their bread and cosseted them long after they had left home, and made sure that any future wife had a difficult time ahead of her. There's no doubt that my grandmother 'spoilt' them, and made her sons think that all women were there to look after them in the way she had.

Yet their role model of a mother was also their undoing, since my father couldn't help but be attracted to a strong-minded and confident woman who refused to conform to the status quo: a woman similar to his mother.

My mother had lost her own mother as a child. When it came to mothering me she had no clear role model to guide her. My mother had learned to stand on her own two feet from a young age, and knew herself to be capable of great resilience. She told me that before she married my father she was rather drawn to his close-knit family, who all seemed to take care of one another. His mother in particular was very welcoming to this rather glamorous, alluring young woman. However, once married, my mother was expected to take over the role of tending to my father's needs. The charm my father had exerted to win my mother quickly evaporated, to be replaced by the demands of a rather selfish, immature young man.

I was always puzzled as to why my mother had chosen to marry a man who required to be mothered so much. Yet I have noticed in countless marriages – even in affluent families where the wife is educated and has achieved certain financial and professional success – a certain expectation that the men should be looked after. In my own childhood it was particularly evident in the working-class families where the men's roles were more clearly defined – they were the earners, the wives were the homemakers. More often than not the wives had little financial independence and few opportunities to escape domestic entrapment.

My father's attraction to my mother was easy to understand. She must have seemed like a breath of fresh air: well dressed, nicely spoken and self-confident. My father thought she was a prize worth winning. But once the wedding ring was on she was expected to become the subservient housewife, with her needs subsumed by his. In the short time in which my mother was married to my father there were fireworks. Their fractious relationship was further undermined by my grandmother's critical attitude to her daughter-in-law who did not seem to 'know her place'. As an archetypal working-class woman, she judged her daughter-in-law on how she mothered her son!

The moment when a woman becomes a mother is a moment of huge transition in her life. Not only is there the new bond with her child, but it also marks a new stage in her relationship with her own mother and her mother-in-law, as they take new places in relation to each other and to society. A mother has become a grandmother; a child has become a mother; it's another rung up on life's ladder. Mixed-up emotions are inevitable. A baby throws a family into turmoil as all its members begin to adjust to their new positions and to the shifts of power within the family structure.

Celia (32) told me:

When I first met the woman who was to be my mother-in-law I was struck by how similar we were. I talked to David

a lot about this but he took a while to accept he had been attracted to me, in part, because I was like his mother. He is very close to her and we have sometimes rowed about her and her involvement in our lives.

I have an affectionate but distant relationship with my own mother. I've been pretty independent from a young age and not really felt I've needed her much. My husband was the last to leave home, spent a lot of time with his mother and I can see exactly why he gets on so well with her. She is great fun and is passionately interested in her children's lives. The comparison between David's family and with my own, fairly hands-off, parents was astonishing to me.

When we were first married I found this level of interest in us a bit bizarre and off-putting. I just couldn't understand how or why she could care so much. She would make assumptions about the way I did things in the house as a way of telling me what she thought I should do. I was pretty defensive because I felt insecure about her – she's a real superwoman! David has a high-powered job, but mine is no less important within our marriage and he respects and admires my work. My mother-in-law once saw David ironing his own shirts and I felt paranoid that she disapproved. She found it hard at first to accept that he cooks as well. On a few occasions when David's parents came to dinner he would cook but we'd pretend I had made it just to avoid her disapproval – even though I was probably imagining it. She has looked after her husband all their married life and I thought that she found it hard to accept how much we share the domestic and childcare arrangements at home.

We have two daughters now and she is a wonderful grandmother. She approves, thank goodness, of my working part-time from home. When our second child was born David decided to go part-time and look after the children to give me a day to work each week. His mother was quite anxious at first as she felt he was endangering his glittering career. In fact, it was very important to him to make a stand for flexible working and he has since gained respect at work for being the only part-time man in his company.

Over and again my mother-in-law has conceded that we have got things right with raising the girls and with the way we work and run our home. She and I are now great friends and have overcome the early difficulties of our relationship. I attribute this to the fact that David became very ill with cancer when he was only 30 and our first child was six months old. He is fully recovered now and we have another daughter. But during his treatment, I needed to visit him every day and I just couldn't cope with looking after a baby too. She got on the first train and came to help me. We had an extraordinary time together. It was awkward to begin with but she just rolled up her sleeves and got on with helping me. She did all the washing and ironing, walked the dog, cooked, cleared up after meals, planned the shopping and looked after Livvy each after-noon so I could make the long journey to and from the hospital. She felt this was a natural extension of loving her son – and it was something practical she could do to help during such a terrible crisis.

Once Livvy had gone to bed in the evening we would

open a bottle of wine and sit down together and talk. As time went by she told me all sorts of things about her own childhood. I felt privileged to be sharing her memories and her thoughts. She showered me with praise and affection, let me cry my terrible fears for my husband on her shoulder, helped me and kept me company during the hardest time of my life.

It was a crisis that bought us close and we both laugh about it now and feel glad that we had the chance to get to know each other. We are united completely in our love for David and I am grateful for her continued role in our lives. For the past few years we have all gone on holiday every summer and although we never recreate the atmosphere of those difficult months, they are always there between us along with an unspoken tolerance, respect and affection.

Not surprisingly, I find that it is the women of the family who usually experience most of the emotional upheaval. The relationships between a mother, her own mother or her mother-in-law can become extremely tense and not always as supportive as they might be. The older women have brought up their own children and usually consider them a success – so their way of raising children is obviously the right way. They find it hard to accept that methods of childcare may have changed, or that someone wants to do things a little differently from the way they did it.

The truth is, friction is normal, disagreements are normal, and hurt and pain are normal, even if it seems terribly unfair. But it strikes at the very core of our beings when our decisions regarding mothering are questioned or criticised, or when we are not supported by those we feel ought to be closest and most understanding of us. You might expect the tension to occur between mothers and their own mothers, but this is not the case in my experience. Where there might have been tension, competition and quarrelling, more often there was understanding and co-operation. It's a big generalisation, but girls tend to have difficult relationships with their mothers in the early years, and grow closer to them as the years go by, especially after they've had children. A new understanding seems to grow up between them, as the new mother realises for the first time what 'motherhood really entails' and what her own mother went through in raising her. The sheer amount of work, dedication and love needed to raise a child hits for the first time when she is in the position of caring for a newborn. It's as though the mother and daughter have at last become equals and it means they grow closer and trust each other.

Where the new mother may readily acknowledge her own mother's experience of caring for her, it tends to be a different matter where her mother-in-law is concerned. The delicate relationship between a new mother and her mother-in-law can be upset in the early days – and often this has long-lasting effects on the family unit as a whole, with grandparents missing out on seeing as much of their grandchildren as they would wish, and grandchildren missing out on the wisdom and love of their father's parents.

I have watched this scenario evolve many times during my years of working with families – usually because problems already existed to do with ownership of the husband/son. You might imagine a possessive mother-in-law wanting to come in and take over the new baby, but in my experience this is rarely the case. It is not the child she wants to control, but the set-up. This is particularly painful when there is already an attitude problem with the son's choice of wife.

Tamara (23) said:

My parents-in-law never liked me. I think they blamed me somehow for ruining their son's life by falling in love and marrying him so young. But we managed to rub along all right and they always seemed to retain their fondness for my husband.

But when Jasmine came along, it was horrible. They just weren't interested. They didn't want to visit, and on the rare occasions when they did they didn't want to hold her. At the same time, at family gatherings, they'd be all over their other son's children. My husband was unbelievably hurt and felt angry that our child was being denied a relationship with her grandparents, however vile they are, through no fault of her own.

I have lost count of the number of times I have been taken to one side by the mother-in-law in a family where I was working. I would listen patiently while she unburdened herself to me, clearly needing to get the criticism off her chest: her daughter-in-law wasn't doing things right, wasn't cooking, cleaning or arranging things correctly. It was obvious what her main concern was: she was worried that her son was not being looked after properly. It was reminiscent of my poor mother and the gift of the bottle of lemonade intended to keep her husband's strength up. Sometimes I have felt that the new mother was being overly sensitive to her mother-in-law, who often just wanted to be part of the new family that had just been formed. An offer to do the cleaning can be seen as an implied criticism of the state of the house; and an offer to cook means the daughter-in-law can't cope.

It's a phenomenon I've witnessed usually in families where the women are fiercely independent and expect to be able to cope with everything and anything by themselves. In other cultures I've worked in, it is traditional to ply a new mother with help and there is no sense that it is undermining her role or implying she is inadequate. In some of the Jewish families I've known, for example, the new mother is inundated with weeks' worth of prepared meals, not just from the immediate family but also from friends and neighbours. These new mothers appreciated the attention and saw it as both supportive and appropriate. They recognised these gestures as expressing the care they deserved from their families at a time when they needed it most.

Gail (39) told me:

I didn't see my in-laws much when my first child was born as we were living abroad. I missed the involvement and support of both our families then, and I was delighted that we moved back home when I was pregnant with our second child. My in-laws came to visit just after the birth of my second child. I was just out of hospital after a difficult delivery. I had two children in nappies, a section scar that wasn't healing and an overwhelming sense of fatigue. One afternoon my in-laws insisted we all go for a walk and, when we passed a wine shop, my mother-in-law asked what we were having for dinner. I hadn't given it a moment's thought, but when I spotted a fishmonger nearby, blurted with some relief, 'Oh, I think we might have salmon.' Fine, she said, 'I'll just go and buy a nice bottle of Chablis.' Despite a new baby, surgery, sleepless nights and hormonal upheaval, my in-laws were treating their visit like a holiday, and I played along by displaying endless good cheer, disguising my pain and looking as if I was coping with everything. As a result, they didn't offer to help in the house or with the children, and when they left after four days, I recall waving as the taxi pulled away, before collapsing to my knees in despair the moment it was out of sight.

At the time I felt angry and let down by my in-laws, but looking back I realise that, because I put on such a brave face, they didn't think I either wanted help or needed it. To some extent we were all paralysed with fear: my fear was of looking weak and losing control; theirs was of interfering or getting something 'wrong' in my apparently perfect system. Yet my in-laws are kind and practical people, and I should simply have *asked* for much-needed help. They would have enjoyed being useful, my toddler would have soaked up the extra attention, and I could have regained some strength, rather than burning every last scrap of it on ill-considered entertaining and thinly veiled resentment. I suppose that even a kind and loving mother-in-law will not always know how to act in a given situation.

There was a happy ending in Gail's case and she learned from this early mistake, but there are plenty of other situations where relationships can break down irretrievably. Mothers who have over-coddled their sons usually can't let go and they contribute to difficulties in the relationships. The main effect usually is that the sons expect to be treated like princes by their wives. This might only come to a head once a baby arrives, as one woman told me:

Catherine (32):

When the baby came, life took a real downturn. Before then, Rob and I had been equal partners. We'd made the most of our twenties, and had got used to a certain quality of life. While we knew that parenthood would come with some constraints, little did we realise quite how restricting it would be in the early days. We had both worked hard at our careers, and as a result we both did a little bit of the housework and a bit of the cooking – although now, when I think back, I realise that I did much more than he did. If Rob so much as washed a cup, I'd thank him and think how terrific he was. I'd had a super cleaner who did the lion's share of the housework, but she was a casualty of the baby. It was difficult to justify the expense when I wanted to go back to work part-time, so I let her go just after I went on maternity leave. What a mistake.

When the baby was born the biggest shock was that Rob suddenly acted as if we had gone back to the 1950s. I had all the childcare to deal with – and Rob stopped helping with the housework. We were both incredibly tired, however Rob would always belittle my exhaustion by pointing out that I wasn't working so I would be able to sleep in the day, but he had no such luxury. Of course, the reality is that there is very little time for catching up on your sleep with a newborn, unless you have a very supportive friend or grandparent to take over for an hour or two. I had neither. I was virtually on my own with Jake from 6.30am to 7pm. As for sleeping in the day, what a joke! Even if I could guarantee Jake's sleep times, there was always so much to be done during the periods when he was in his cot. I barely had time to make a cup of tea, let alone indulge in the sort of lazy days that Rob implied.

The nights were awful. Rob is such a deep sleeper that generally when Jake woke for a night-time feed, Rob would simply groan, roll over and go back to sleep. It was always me up with our baby, feeding and settling him. Then in the morning, despite the fact that I might have had very little consistent sleep Rob would moan on about how tired he was. One of the worst aspects was he showed so little interest in Jake. If I asked him to change Jake, or wind him, Rob would do so with minimum enthusiasm and always hand him back with the words 'You're better at it anyway.' Of course I was better at it – I had a great deal more practice, and Rob had very little by choice!

A visit from my mother-in-law, Mary, was the catalyst for bringing all this to a head. Jake was about eight weeks old and I felt completely drained. I was terribly unhappy, and resented Rob's lack of understanding but had yet to address it with him. We were rowing regularly but the penny hadn't quite dropped. Rob just dismissed our quarrels as me being hormonal!

I had been up twice in the night with Jake, and had spent two hours attempting to tidy up the house, knowing that Mary would disapprove of the chaos that had become our norm. Mary had been driving me loopy since she had arrived, asking questions about how Rob was finding it. Was he tired? Eating properly? Finding time to see his friends? As we walked back from the market, weighed down with produce, she asked me what I was planning to cook for everyone that evening. It didn't even occur to her that perhaps Rob might cook.

A couple of hours later, I was standing in the kitchen preparing supper, having just expressed some milk and tackled some of the repetitive domestic jobs which were my sole responsibility. I was almost too tired to think. Rob came in and plonked himself down on the sofa to talk to his father. His mother immediately poured him a beer. He wanted a cold one, so she exchanged it for one in the fridge. She took him some crisps and began to ask about his day. I stood there trying not to cry. What on earth had I let myself in for? Suddenly I saw the future. I had to make Rob see that I was not his mother. Life was not going to follow the same pattern as his childhood. I was not going to mother both Rob and Jake. I couldn't help blaming my mother-in-law for making him so unsupportive, useless and downright selfish.

My best friend gave me the best advice. Don't try to explain it to him, show him what it's like. I had been winding down the breast-feeding, and two weeks later arranged to spend a weekend with a friend in a lovely spa hotel. Rob would have the weekend to himself and Jake. Rob had complained at first and then become complacent at the prospect of being able to cope. Jake was taking a bottle happily and I expressed plenty of milk. I left Rob some very precise instructions, secure in the knowledge that Jake was a pretty easy baby by then, and in quite a fixed routine. I was worrying enormously about Jake, but when I weakened my friend rallied me. The first hour was fine, apparently! But after that 'my boys' stumbled. I spoke to Rob during the afternoon and he sounded hassled, and complained that he hadn't had a chance to eat anything since I left. At 11pm, he rang to say that Jake had taken over an hour to take his feed and only just settled. He hadn't managed to bath Jake, and Rob still hadn't eaten anything. He rang me at 6am and sounded quite desperate. Jake had woken at 2am, and cried off and on for two hours. I promised I would be home by the afternoon but, satisfied that Jake was having an adequate amount to drink, I did not race back. By the time I got back after lunch Rob was on the verge of tears. He was unshaven, shocked, hungry and pathetically grateful to see me. I was relieved to see that Jake appeared none the worse for his experience and I felt incredibly empowered. I dispatched Rob to the super-market, with instructions to do the weekly shop. On his return, I asked him to make supper while I looked after Jake. He gratefully complied. That evening we bathed Jake together and for the first time Rob seemed to really engage. He actually wanted to learn how to do it. Three nights later, still feeling encouraged by the weekend and the profound effect it had had on Rob, I organised a babysitter and we went out to supper together.

Without crying, I explained to him quite how difficult I had found his attitude during the first months of Jake's life. I told him that if he took me for granted our marriage would not be a happy one. Rob immediately began to demonstrate that he would try harder. Of course, we both had to work at it. Not least I had to recognise that occasionally making Rob a drink or pairing his socks was not an indication of my domestic subservience, but rather a reflection of the nice things you do for one another in a marriage. Rob would cook for me two or three times a week, and when he got home he would try to ask about my day. Perhaps the very best aspect was seeing his relationship with Jake flourish. As he became more involved with looking after Jake, and more confident, Jake rewarded him with fabulous gurgles and chuckles.

The next time my parents-in-law came to stay they were astonished to find Rob on his hands and knees changing nappies and fully involved. Mary kept making comments about 'modern fatherhood', and how Rob's father hadn't changed a nappy in his life. I tried not to be rattled and was gratified that Rob seemed almost embarrassed by his mother's comments. When she tried to mother him, he responded by helping me. It's funny really, that it took seeing Mary in action for me to realise quite how detached and spoilt Rob had become. I suppose I should thank her that it was she who made me see the light!

There is an old saying which, like most adages, contains a great deal of truth: a son's a son 'til he takes a wife – but a daughter is a daughter all of your life.

The subject of motherhood should not be limited to women. During my decades of looking after babies I have seen many different kinds of fathers. Celia, above, realised when she met her mother-in-law that they were actually very similar. We women joke about men wanting to marry their mothers – perhaps to replicate the intense love and care they received, or maybe just to be sure their socks get washed. But the relationship between a man and his mother is a crucial one. It can affect his choice of wife and, as we saw from Catherine and Rob's story above, it can affect the role he unconsciously expects his wife to take on once a baby arrives.

I heard a very positive story from Bill about his mother and the way she shaped his life. He has had to resist his mother's desire to replicate his own upbringing in her grandsons and this is a constantly recurring theme:

Bill (43):

It's not a fashionable thing to admit to, but I had a very happy and stable childhood. I was very close to my mother. She was tough but fun. Games would be created out of nothing and there was always a lot of laughter and silliness at home. I had three brothers and Dad was running his own business. Mum had total responsibility for the house and for us. She stayed at home until I was seven but then returned to work specifically to earn enough to privately educate us all which was something my dad didn't believe in but she was passionate about and determined to make happen. It was hard because I had to get to school by myself, at the age of seven. I had a key to get in the house after school. Mum would have prepared snacks for my brothers and me and we would eat and do our homework together until she got home at about 5.30pm.

School was very important to Mum. She pushed us to work hard and I knew I was meant to do well. My brothers and I now have good jobs and are based in Europe – I know my mum is very proud of what we've achieved and her vital role in providing the education and environment that made it possible. She actually was very successful in her work in a trendy architect's office. But the day the last child – me – had finished at school, she handed in her notice at work, to her colleagues' horror. She had achieved what she'd set out to do and that was that for her.

During my school years and beyond both Mum and Dad have shown great interest in everything I have done, in my friends and my girlfriends. Sometimes they've been overly interested and I have resented it – when I got my first job in an accountancy firm my mum wanted to help me choose my suits. I did actually need her help but I didn't like her assuming I did! They also gave me sensible advice when I was in my early twenties about buying a house and managing my finances with care. I just wanted to enjoy my newfound freedom and salary. It was well meant, though, and they have been enthusiastic and supportive of my decisions and working life.

When I was 28 I met Kelly. She has an in-built strength and capability just like my mother and I suppose that's no coincidence. It was very important to me that my parents, especially my mother, liked her and could see what a great person she was. The first introduction went very well and they seemed to click and get on famously. The trouble came when we quickly got engaged and were planning our wedding. My mum's conservatism kicked in then and she actually took me out in order to ask me if I was quite sure about Kelly and, in other words, was she really good enough for her precious son? I was shocked because it seemed obvious to me how happy I was and how right for me Kelly was. Mum has since admitted that this was a mistake but it hurt at the time.

Our first son was born when I was 35. I took huge pride in presenting him to my mother for the first time. There was something very tribal about showing him off – 'look what I have done'. Her reaction was of complete joy and she is a wonderful grandmother, entertaining her grand-sons with the same silly songs and made-up games that she played with my brothers and me. At the same time a certain level of interference has returned. There are references to how things were done 30 years ago. Kelly works part-time from home and my mother stresses her huge approval that the boys are not in childcare at all. She showers Kelly with praise for the way she is mothering our sons, but I wonder what she would say if Kelly had decided to work outside the home and we had put the children into a nursery.

My mother has raised her own children successfully and this now makes her cling to her methods as being the only way, which is sometimes difficult to cope with. Sometimes, I think that she would like us to buy the house next door to her and Dad and to send the boys to the same school I went to. It is easy to see why she wants to repeat the pattern but it's very important to me that my boys have their own lives.

As a son and a father I have realised that children start at the age of nought totally dependent on the parents who are at the centre of their world. Very gradually they move away from their parents, further out into the world, with protective hands still holding on until they are ready to go on their own. At the end of a parent's life, children need to be able to let them go and to fully live their own lives. The cycle seems very clear to me and I expect and hope that my sons will be equipped to leave home after their education is completed, and that letting them go will feel natural and right. Then the focus of my life will again be my marriage and I am looking forward to being in the position my own parents are now where they can travel together, enjoy each other's company and be without the responsibility for their children.

Bestselling author Steve Biddulph writes about the role of mothers of sons in his book *Raising Boys*. He acknowledges that many mothers feel more confident with a baby girl. 'They feel they would intuitively know what to do with her. But a boy! After the birth of a son, it's not unusual for a mother to exclaim in horror, "I don't know what to *do* with a boy".' It can be unknown territory for a mother and cause her to take her hands off the parental wheel. William's story below partly illustrates this – that four boys born one after the other are finally followed by the much-desired daughter, who receives considerably more involvement and closeness from the mother.

William (45):

I was the fourth boy of five children. My mother really wanted a daughter. We were brought up in rural Devon and Mum was a full-time homemaker. Dad was a rep and on the road a lot so we didn't see very much of him. My mother suffered from postnatal depression after almost all of her five children. It wasn't an acknowledged condition then, of course, but she found things very difficult. My two oldest brothers spent a lot of time at my grandparents' house and they were there to help us all. It was a happy and peaceful childhood on the whole. We boys had huge freedom and would go off on adventures all the time. The attitude was that you could do whatever you wanted provided the police never knocked on Mum's door.

None of us was pushed at school. We were expected to leave home at 18, no matter what. My brothers promptly disappeared at 18 into the forces or the merchant marine. I left school at 18 and went to London for three years. I worked there for a couple of years before training as a teacher. After I left home there wasn't much contact. I wasn't close to my mum. She didn't have time for that sort of thing and I don't think she knew how to build an intimate relationship with us boys. It was different for my sister, though. My mother wasn't demonstrative with us and never told us she was proud of us. I never brought girlfriends home and kept my life private. It was really a continuation of childhood – as long as you're not in trouble it doesn't matter what you get up to.

I met Eliza when I was 31 and we got engaged one New Year's Eve. On New Year's Day I phoned my mother to tell her the news. It was a short conversation. Straight afterwards one of my brothers mentioned to her that Eliza was a Roman Catholic. Three days later the phone rang at dawn and my mother was screaming down the phone at me that Eliza (whom she'd never met) was a gold-digger who would hold my career back, that she wasn't good enough for me and that it wasn't too late for me to change my mind. She then wrote me a letter voicing her unshakeable view that Catholics had lots of children and came from huge clans that would 'suck me in' and 'get their claws' into me. She was fearful of a mythical powerful extended family.

I have not spoken to her since that early morning phone call. The wedding invitation was ignored. Christmas cards came for a few years and then stopped. When our daughter Helen was born we sent photos. There was no response. My older brother still visits our parents and told me that my mother has the photos of baby Helen that she hides from my dad. My daughter is now nine and looks a lot like I did at that age.

My mother is now in her mid-seventies. I hear news of my parents from my brothers. I feel very sad for her as she has missed out on her granddaughter. Helen had a family tree project at school when she was about eight and we had to explain to her that we didn't see her other grandparents. Helen is very close to Eliza's parents (who aren't remotely clannish, incidentally!) and we see them most weeks and go on holiday with them. It's a comfort that she has one set of grandparents at least who love her, know her and are involved in her life. Not surprisingly, I have gone the other way as a parent from my own upbringing. I'm now a deputy head teacher working with children every day. I'm a very hands-on dad, interested in everything my daughter does without intruding on her privacy. I can't imagine a circumstance in which I would not always have her in my life.

The mother of sons has a very distinct role as her child develops and moves away from the bosom and into the world. Biddulph advises mothers of boys that their role needs to change as their sons grow up – from caring for them as babies and toddlers, to encouraging them and nurturing their sense of self, to gentle guidance as they gain responsibility and freedom. One teenage boy might still consent to a cuddle with Mum now and again, while another finds it too intrusive. One woman told me about a conversation over a glass of wine with her boyfriend's mother. It went like this:

Mother: You are so lucky to have him, you know.
Girlfriend (amicably): Yes, I know. He's fantastic.
Mother: You get to see his bottom.
Girlfriend: Excuse me?
Mother: He had the most gorgeous bottom when he was a baby and I haven't seen it for years. I'm sure it's horrible and hairy now, but, still, I used to love it . . .

The girlfriend went on to marry the man with the marvellous bottom, but only when she had her first son was she finally able to understand what her mother-in-law had been saying. The idea that not far into the future the physical closeness women enjoy with their baby boys will come to an end is a poignant one.

A whole chapter of this book is devoted to the question of friendship between mothers and daughters. Yet sons can often enjoy a closeness with their mothers. I have seen this over and over again when a boy loses his father either through death or abandonment. He may take on a protective role with his mother, perhaps trying to be 'the man of the house' or simply from concern and love. In a recent survey over 36 months, of children who came from homes where there was domestic violence, every single son over the age of 14 attempted to protect his mother. Some 62 per cent were injured in the process.

Ricky (36) told me his story:

I was brought up in Australia. My mother is British and had been on holiday when she met and married my father. They had two sons. My father was violent towards my mother and, when I was four, she left him and they divorced. She took my brother and me to live on a farm where we became part of a big extended family who lived there too and gave Mum the security and support she needed.

We saw Dad every week and a few years later my mother met and married Peter. Thankfully, he is very different from my Dad – an intelligent but impractical man. He is very good for Mum and they are still happily married. When I was nine we moved to Amsterdam. Mum had been a successful corporate florist but couldn't work in pre-EC Holland without a work permit. She is a resourceful woman and kept busy doing courses, community work and pursuing her own cultural education. When I was 12 I started at boarding-school in England where I settled in and was very happy. Holidays were split between Australia and Holland.

Coming from divorced parents, each with their own values and morals, I think I quickly learned that there was more than one way of doing everything. Once my mother felt that my brother and I had grown up and developed our own view of the world, she told us about the darker side of her marriage to my father. I had no memories of the time at all but I wasn't surprised. He is a very successful and powerful man, who has often been a bully and excessively aggressive in achieving his aims. I felt disappointed in him. I think my mother has often been naïve and unrealistic about her expectations of a perfect, happy life. It's not what you have, but how much you enjoy what you have that makes happiness.

My mother and Peter moved to England when I was in my last year at school. I spent lots of happy time with them after that. When I was 29 I met Anna and we married a few years later. She and my mother got on well although they were very different people. After three years of marriage I discovered that my wife was having an affair and we separated. It was very painful. I didn't tell my mother the whole story. To everyone, my brother excepted, Anna and I were separating because we wanted different things: I wanted a family and to live in the country; she wanted to stay in a city and wasn't ready for children.

I felt that if I told my mother the truth about my divorce she would worry about me and it would bring up painful memories of her own divorce, from which she has never recovered in some ways. My brother and I have emotionally supported our mother for a long time now. We worry about her and we talk about how we can help her.

My mother's best friend is my godmother and I've known her all my life. I never had cause to call on her help in a godmotherly way but, when I was 18 or 19, she asked me if I needed any religious or spiritual guidance. When I um-ed and ah-ed a bit and finally turned down the offer she heaved a sigh of relief and suggested we went to the pub. We've been very close since and I live near her and her family and see them all the time.

I still really want to find the right woman to share my life with and have a family. I am having a 'new start' right now and have followed my dream of living by the sea and setting up my own business. I am very jealous of people who have children. I have wanted them for about five years now. But you can't do it on your own, can you?

A son is as capable as a daughter of showing solidarity with his mother when a marriage is in trouble. Oscar's story below shows a remarkable insight into his parents' marriage and his compassion for his mother when tragedy struck their family:

As the story goes, my father was a persistent man. He had met my mum at Oxford University where he was reading Mathematics and she had an administrative role. He was so determined to take her out that after a while she finally relented to his request for a date, and a short while after that they were married.

She was 26 when she had me. I have never doubted her love, as she did everything for me. When I was two I was presented with a baby brother, Louis. I remember being really fond of him, and I have seen old cine-film of him toddling along, with me clutching his hand.

Growing up I remember my dad being quite awkward

with everyone: my mum, her friends, her family and us. He was very competitive and didn't let me win at games. It wasn't all bad; he did read stories to me and play a bit, but I think he always had a tough time expressing his emotions. They had a hard marriage. She found him possessive, secretive and very withdrawn. I think in retrospect she suspected he was having an affair, but she never mentioned it at the time. She told me she once ran away to her parents, but they just sent her back and told her to make a go of it. They weren't being cruel; they were just trying to get her to make the best choices, although this probably wasn't the best choice.

The worst ebb of her life was finding out that Louis was terminally ill when he was only a few years old. Not only was she faced with losing her son, but she found my dad increasingly withdrawn and even harder to live with than before. Louis finally died at home in my parents' bed. It was my seventh birthday. I remember her often just coming into my room at night and holding on to me, sobbing. I was quite bewildered but she remembers me patting her back, trying to reassure her.

I only understand the loss she has faced since I became a father myself. Until you have children of your own, you view these issues compassionately although with detach-ment. I simply cannot imagine suffering the grief of losing a child. I really feel for her.

My dad couldn't deal with the loss at all. He would disappear for hours, and even days at a time, and my mum just put on a brave face most of the time and tried to get on with life. She is quite traditional. She believes marriage is everything. In today's alienated culture this is hard to grasp.

This stilted relationship went on for years and years. I don't think I bear any scars of this difficult time as I was lucky to have uncles, aunts and cousins around as well as my mum, who tried to be as strong as she could.

When I was 18, my father finally left. After all these years of toing and froing, it came as a shock to my mother, but as a relief to me. I remember saying 'Good. Finally' to her, when she came to my university halls of residence to break the news.

In the years after that, she has been managing quite well on her own. She has never remarried, although I sometimes think it might be a good move for her. I hardly see my dad any more. He gets in touch once a year, but that's about that. My mum has loads of friends and keeps herself busy doing voluntary work and social activities. Once in a while though she does crack, and calls up in tears. I think she finds life on her own very hard. Some of her friends are divorced too, so luckily she isn't the only one (appearances are very important to her: a certain way of life, brand names, doing the 'right' thing). She never wants to spend money on herself. She prefers to spend it on me, my wife and our children. We see her a lot, and involve her in our family life a lot too. Although she sometimes irritates me, I love her to pieces. I wish she would be a little happier in her skin.

There's a very funny John Hegley poem that goes something like: 'Men live with their mothers for years and years'. It brings a clichéd image to mind of the dysfunctional male, over-protected and spoiled by a dominant mother. Unable to form a relationship of his own, he lives within her walls until her death leaves him alone, probably depressed or with mental health problems, unable to boil an egg for himself. The truth is often very far from this. Peter (45) spoke to me about his mother, who lives in the same apartment block, though in a different flat from him:

I am an only child. My mother worked before I was born but gave up work to look after me. My childhood with my parents was generally a happy one. The main areas of conflict with my mother were about staying out late with the wrong crowd, and schoolwork. I found this annoying because I was happy to study but my mother wouldn't leave me be. She was very ambitious for me and always wanted me to succeed. Sometimes I felt like there was way too much control going on. She was competitive on my behalf. I'm now an investment banker so it must all have paid off, I suppose.

I was closer to my mother than to my father and so there were more emotional conflicts with her. I didn't go to either parent with problems – in fact, I can't really recall any problems. I felt loved by my mother, but I found her love interfering. Her world seemed to revolve around me more than it did my father. My mother was overwhelming on occasions – very hands-on, almost too involved. She seemed to have a fear of something bad happening and was very over-protective, both physically and emotionally. If my mother had worked outside the home, she'd have been less involved with me. She, to some extent, lived through me.

My late teens at home were a bit messy, but once I left home at 18 it became fine, although the separation period had its ups and downs. Our relationship has got a lot better over time and we've accepted each other more. She's necessarily less hands-on now. She used to say, 'You should be doing this, or that, etc.' and now she doesn't. I spent my teenage years fighting my mother's involvement, but now I'm able to put down boundaries.

I moved into my flat when it unexpectedly became available, initially as a temporary investment opportunity. But after my father died a few years ago, the proximity to my mother has resulted in it being a convenience for her as it meant I was around when she was going through a difficult period. It's also a great place and suited my needs. I sometimes feel embarrassed to admit that I live that close to my 80-year-old mother! But when she was seriously ill last year I was very glad to be so near to her as it meant I could easily take her to and from hospital appointments and make sure she was being looked after. As an only child it is a significant responsibility and not one that is easy to resent or walk away from.

I'm single at the moment but I would ultimately like to have children. I instinctively feel it should be part of your life if it can be. I have been too busy working so far and feel that the right relationship must come first. My dad was in his late thirties when I was born so that does refocus your thoughts. I am still single probably because I have unrealistic expectations. My mother cooked and cleaned for my dad and me. I admit that I have increasingly become a bit of a control freak and I am not good at allowing any woman to do these things if she's not 'doing it right'. I think over the years that I've convinced myself that the 'right girl' may be just on the other side of the fence, but I've no doubt sometimes not engaged enough in a relationship and moved it onwards. I've also allowed it to be subordinated to work and my obsessive triathlon training sessions. There's been a misplaced fear of being trapped or having to give up my lifestyle. My mother attempted to influence my choice of girlfriend and she would let me know what she thought of them after a while. Now I think she's in more of a hurry for me to settle down but ten or fifteen years ago she was much harder to please.

I definitely assess potential partners as mothers and a part of that is the 'emotional generosity' in a woman that my mother had for me. But my ideal partner would be less anxious than my mother was. I would expect a partner to work, to bring in income, but from what I can gather, my father wanted my mother to look after me. So until I get there, who knows what I will feel. I do think that the world of work should be changed to accommodate working mothers. As a businessman, I find that maternity leave and flexi-hours can make life difficult but I believe that they are a necessity. Long hours and the presenteeism culture are not the most productive. We can deal with maternity leave and so on more easily here than in other parts of Europe. I know high-powered women who had six months' leave but were back within three to safeguard their career and their position in the office. This sort of pressure is wrong.

I suppose I would discuss the upbringing of children before committing to a partner. And I just don't think I'd be likely to fall in love with someone who wasn't the right person to have children with, but the future always holds a few surprises.

Not all men, of course, form relationships with women. The National Survey of Sexual Attitudes and Lifestyle undertook research between 1989 and 1990 of nearly 19,000 people in the UK. It found it virtually impossible to arrive at precise numbers of gay men and women in the UK, but they are estimated to form a significant percentage of the population. In the past few decades the atmosphere surrounding sexual preference has become increasingly tolerant, thank goodness. The mother whose son tells her he is gay may struggle with the news as she adjusts to the reality that she is unlikely to be attending a wedding or welcoming a grandchild, but she is less likely than ever before to be ashamed to tell her friends or fear ostracism as a result. One friend welcomed her son's announcement and made the most of shopping trips and weekly lunches. She saw a world beyond her own relatively narrow one as her son introduced her to his partner and friends and felt that her life was enriched. I heard a fascinating story from Robbie (38) who lives in America now but who talked to me about his experience with his sexuality and how his family is affected:

I was the oldest child in a very secure and loving family. We were always close and when I was growing up they supported me in all my decisions and allowed me to pursue my interests. I was quite private I suppose because I struggled during most of my late teens and twenties with my sexuality. I had my first homosexual experience at the age of 14 with my German exchange partner whom my sister was madly pursuing! It didn't lead to anything further for a long time and I dated plenty of girls. Looking back, the girls I chose were a bit like me – brainy and not very good-looking! I chose them all for their friendship and person-ality although sex would eventually be a problem and the relationships would end, mostly disastrously. I have many female friends now and value them enormously.

I know that when I was in my early twenties my mother asked my sister if she thought I might be gay. I think she was respecting my privacy by not asking me directly and at that stage I wasn't sure at all. I wanted to have a family and a conventional life, but it always felt wrong being with a woman. I finally came to terms with being gay when I was 30. It was a very difficult and long struggle because I really wanted to replicate my own happy family but I couldn't go on being unhappy and lonely.

I invited my parents and sister over to Rome where I was living at the time and sat them down over coffee to tell them I was bisexual. This was mostly true as I did try occasionally to form a sexual relationship with a woman, but I wanted to break the news gently to my family and I thought this would make it easier for them. There were lots of tears and hugs but complete acceptance from everyone. My parents told me I was loved unconditionally and that nothing mattered more than my happiness.

I was delighted and tremendously relieved. Because I'd told them I was bisexual I think they hoped I might eventually tip towards the female, but they accepted this wasn't going to happen when I met and fell in love with my current partner, Harry. We have been together now for the past six years and he's been welcomed into the family.

We live in America and are currently in the process of fathering a child together. My sperm are being implanted into donated eggs that will then go into a surrogate mother. Harry will then adopt the child or children and we will bring him or her up together. We have thought long and hard about this decision, and looked at it from every angle. Many people are shocked by it; some even feel it is wrong for two men to raise a child together. But I'm sure we've given it a lot more thought than many heterosexual couples who only need a slip-up in contraception to make a baby. I have wanted to be a father for as long as I can remember and Harry and I will be totally dedicated to our child and its welfare. Harry will give up work permanently and I will be the breadwinner.

I've talked openly to my mother and father about this decision at all its stages, and I think this has helped them to appreciate how much time and thought have gone into it. At first my mother worried that it was unnatural and that my relationship with Harry might not sustain a child as well. But as the process has gathered momentum she has accepted it. She knows that parents are the people who are there for a child and she wants to provide the child with loving grandparents. There will be cousins, aunts and uncles as well, who all support us. My mother's only sadness now is that her new grandchild will be on the other side of the world from her. I have been lucky to be able to

talk so openly to my parents and to have received so much
love and acceptance from them.

Not everyone has Robbie's good fortune in having such loving
parents. A woman told me how she could accept her son was
gay once he was in a stable relationship, but found his earlier
years of promiscuity frightening and abhorrent. She was
estranged from him during those years but since he has 'settled
down' they have become close again.

For many young men the loss of parental support at a
crucial stage of their lives, combined with the negative effects
of prejudice and discrimination, can lead to anxiety, depression and self-harm. One in five gay men has made a suicide
attempt, according to the largest ever UK survey of the mental
health of lesbian, gay and bisexual people published in 2003
by the mental health charity, Mind. It also reports high rates
of dependency on drugs and alcohol among the gay population. This is attributed to the stress of coming to terms with
their sexuality, as described by Robbie above, and to society's
attitude towards them and direct experience of being discrimi-
nated against. Between 25 and 60 per cent of gay people seek
counselling at some stage in their lives. It seems we have a
long way to go as a society towards accepting the individuality
of our young people.

Research from Finland in May 2002 found that giving birth
to a son can shorten a woman's lifespan compared to having
a daughter. The research team thought that the physiological
demands of giving birth to a heavy son might explain the
research, but also that a beneficial effect of having daughters
would be their availability to assist with domestic tasks. Many

mothers of sons might laughingly concur with this. Years of washing and cooking and caring for boys who don't lift a finger to help must take its toll. Although, as I found in my own researches, there are mothers like my own mother's mother-in-law who take a tremendous pride in waiting on them hand and foot. Without doubt it's a very special relationship and any woman who marries a man with a 'special' mum, as my own mother did, knows that they are taking on emotional baggage.

There's a final irony to all this that makes me laugh every time. My mother never mothered a man in her whole life. And yet, where men are concerned, whenever I am in a relationship I absolutely love mothering men! So it seems that although my grandmother's influence wasn't big in my life, it comes out in me when men are concerned. It seems that such an instinct can skip a generation.

Chapter 8

❋

The
Twilight
Years

❋

In the autumn of 1993 it was groundhog day at my parents' house. My mother had decided she wanted to redecorate the kitchen with her favourite kind of flowery wallpaper. There she was at the top of the stepladder this time. The pencil skirt was gone and she was in skintight jeans. I was sitting in the rocking chair directing her – a bit to the left, a bit to the right – as she hung the paper. My stepfather was in charge of the paste and he called out, 'Lena, are we really up to this in our twilight years?' She answered him straight back: 'Speak for yourself! I'm a long way off my twilight years.' Two days later we'd achieved the hanging of the wallpaper, in spite of the uneven walls. I was climbing into a taxi on my way to the airport and on to Hong Kong for work. There were the usual hugs and kisses, but when I looked back to wave at her, I suddenly got a lump in my throat. She looked so small and frail and fragile. I put that thought to the back of my mind, but two months later came the phone call.

My mother had been diagnosed with cancer. She was 54.

For five years she was treated with many different kinds of chemotherapy drug, endured radiotherapy and suffered terribly from pain and from the side effects of the treatment. One day, shortly before her death, we were walking round Edinburgh together. We stopped at a shop window to look at a beautiful coat. My mother had always been like a little girl about clothes, she loved pretty things and always looked fabulous. I asked her if she wanted the coat but when I looked into her eyes that day I saw that the sparkle had gone from them. She didn't want the coat, but I insisted on buying it for her. I hustled her into the shop, had her measured for it and paid. It would be ready to collect in two weeks' time. Even then, we both knew she would never wear that coat.

Later on that day we went into our favourite place, the George Hotel, for tea. We'd gone there together for 20 years and during all that time the place had never changed. The walls were the same colour – I think they still are. We sat at the table we always sat at together. I looked down at her hands, clenched tightly around her coffee cup. Her hands were scarred to bits from all the drips and injections that had been made during her cancer treatment. I tried to joke with her about the dust on the skirting boards and how the waiter's trousers could do with an iron. Things we always laughed at together. But that day she couldn't manage even a smile. Her eyes were hollow and empty. The cancer had spread to her throat by then and I knew that she was in terrible pain. At the hospital the previous day I'd been outside her room when I overheard her begging the nurses for more morphine. She didn't want me to see her suffering.

Later that night I took her home and tucked her up in bed,

glad to be caring for her myself. She looked across the room at me and said, 'Gina, I'm worried about you.' I dismissed her worry as soon as she'd uttered it. 'But who will look after you once I'm gone?' she asked. I wasn't having any of this and reassured her that she would be around for a long time. But we both knew that wasn't true. She was dying and there wasn't much time left for us. 'Sometimes I think I've loved you too much, I should have let you go,' she said. And I knew that night that it was true – she *had* loved me too much in a way. I realised that night that there would be no twilight years for my mother and me. I knew I was about to lose the best mother anyone could have asked for, the best friend I'd ever had and, in some ways, the baby I never had. There are no words to express how I felt that night. I clenched my fists tightly because I had to be strong. Every part of my body was rigid when I buried my face in the pillow. I cried for hours and hours yet I never made a sound because I didn't want to disturb her sleep.

Two weeks later I sat by her hospital bed and she urged me to go and write my book. She died later that day and I followed her final advice as I always did. I wrote my book, and went on to write ten more. But it wasn't until I came to write *Good Mother Bad Mother*, my most personal book to date, that I began to realise the extent of her influence upon me. She didn't always get things right but she did the best she could and that is all anyone can ask. It seems to me that the best thing a mother can do is to ensure that many years down the line she is a friend to her child. It's easy to love a baby, but the challenge of motherhood is in loving the toddler, the teenager and the grown adult your child becomes. If you can look that child in the eye when he or she is grown and feel the love there between you; know you have done the best you could; and forgive yourself for the mistakes you have made, then you've done a great job.

A year to the day after my mother died, I went home. I lay on my bed and cried for four hours. I cried like a wild animal for all I had lost. I was as noisy that night as I had been silent the previous year. I survived that first year by working incredibly hard with many wonderful mothers and babies. Those mothers took me into their homes and let me care for their precious babies. They valued me and loved me back. I have survived the past six years, of course, and as I write this book I see how much I've taken from my mother. Her advice to me was always to be strong, to turn the other cheek and walk away; to stand by my beliefs and have confidence in myself. I may not have had those twilight years with her, but everything I have achieved is thanks to her and I am grateful for every moment that we had.

This book came about because of the current climate surrounding parenting. I speak to thousands of mothers every year and my website has become a thriving forum for debate and discussion. I have heard at first hand about the doubts and fears that plague mothers today. I wanted to try and address some of the most pressing issues and to share my own experiences.

Many contributions to this book have been from women in their twenties and thirties. Their insight into early motherhood is invaluable, but I wanted to hear from older women as well. The myth of the wise woman is prevalent in cultures around the world. I have worked in households in many different countries where the grandmothers ruled the roost. While working with mothers and babies, I also listened to the grandmothers. Life keeps changing and progress is made but we must never toss aside the values we learned from the generation above. Yesterday's mothers are as important as today's and tomorrow's. In some cultures, they are attributed with the wisdom of experience by the younger members of the family and by the community at large. In the UK and other Western countries, the elderly are not always treated with similar respect; they are seen by some as a burden on society. Our culture idolises youth and it is the young who drive the fashion and music industries, who are the voices the media and literature of the day hold in highest esteem.

Mothers struggling today with the dilemmas of motherhood – those who ask themselves 'Am I a good mother?' – cannot afford to ignore the voices of the generation above. Their experiences might not be the same as those of our generation, but the bond between mother and child is timeless and what they have to tell us deserves to be heard as much as the voices of the young. After all, every mother of a toddler will one day be the mother of a teenager. That teenager will grow up and eventually leave home and set up their own family unit. This may seem years away for many readers, but hearing the reflections of older women can help young mums focus on the long-term view of parenting.

Women in their twenties and thirties have a great deal more choice available to them than their mothers had. But with choice come doubts and insecurities that the previous generation simply did not have. The sad effect of feminism that I have seen over and again is that the grandmothers of today find it difficult to relate to their daughters' lives and to some modern child-rearing practices. They have limited insight into the freedom that is, thankfully, now available to young women. A distance may grow up between the generations because of this freedom. A woman of 30 with a new baby is likely to have spent the previous decade financially independent, satisfied and stimulated by a rewarding career and free to enjoy the pleasures of travel, sexual liberation and a broad view of the world. The loss of this can contribute to the shock of motherhood discussed above.

Vera (58) told me about her experiences and feelings of motherhood now her daughters are grown up:

The happiest time of my life was when I was at home caring for my two daughters during their pre-school years. I lived in a very close community. The neighbours mostly had children the same age as mine, attending the same nursery schools and playgroups. We helped each other and everyone chipped in when new babies arrived or people were having difficulties. My mum was a tremendous help. She didn't live nearby but would pay long visits. She helped out around the house and she could single-handedly cope with both the children. We were on the same wavelength regarding the upbringing of children.

My daughters are now 32 and 29. The hardest time for me came when I realised that I wasn't needed by them very much any more. They were in their late teens and still living at home. They depended on me for the practical things but they were preparing to leave home and their focus was outwards, on the world beyond my front door.

The process of them both leaving home took several

years because they were three years apart in age. I knew that I would be entering into a new stage of my own life once they'd gone but I found the period of years it took to get there very difficult and sometimes painful. Once they had both left for university I was able to make my marriage – luckily a very happy one – the main focus of my life again, but it took me time to think about what I wanted for myself and for the rest of my own life.

I have stayed close to both my girls. For a period of about 10 years, during their twenties, they were very much absorbed by their university life, travelling and getting their first jobs. They didn't share very much with me during this time. Probably this was a case of generation gap. When I was in my mid-twenties I was bringing up two children. For them these years were about freedom and lack of responsibility.

Since they have established their careers and both made committed relationships, they have come back to my level again and we are now very close – but in a new way. Responsibility and maturity has given them an insight into my life and, with their own marriage and long-term relationship, they seem to have a fresh perspective on their parents' marriage. As a mother it's incredibly rewarding to see your children happy with their full-time work and satisfied in their relationships. I feel that once they have their own children that will fulfil my own sense of what having children is all about. You raise them, you send them out into the world and you hope and long for their happiness and fulfilment.

Things have worked out for my family and I feel so

lucky. My mum died when she was 90 and I was ready to let her go, just as she was ready to leave me. We had those twilight years you are talking about. By then I was happily married and she knew my daughters very well. I was 53 and ready to step up the ladder.

I very much want to be a grandmother. I hope I won't push myself forward once I am. I hope I will respect my daughters' choices and the relationship they have with their in-laws. I do live near both my girls but I don't intend to give up my own life and take on their childcare responsibilities although I want to help and support them. My marriage and my own life are my priority right now. I say that, but who knows how I'll feel when presented with my first grandchild!

Cass is 65 and has two children and two grandchildren. Her life has not been easy and she told me about her mother and how her own parenting was affected by her childhood. I was interested in how friendship has become such an important part of her relationship with her children. Her story explains why:

I was the youngest of four children – the mistake! My mother was very self-sacrificing and very hard working. I don't remember her ever playing with us, or ever having any one-to-one time with her. She never read to me and there was no quality time. I was one of the kids and we all lacked emotional attention. There was so much for her to do domestically and she was always in the kitchen. She never ate with us apart from on Sundays. My dad was in the

Navy during the war and was then a policeman. Later he started work as a rep for a chocolate company. Our house was always full of chocolate!

Education was pretty cursory. My mum always said she had no worries about me and I'd 'do good'. She introduced me to everyone as 'my baby' which I didn't like at all. I left home as soon as I was physically able and I got married at 23. My mother had stopped liking me years before that. As the youngest of four I went into the rebellious 1950s when my older brother and sisters were more conventional and settled. I was a beatnik, listened to Elvis and went out with lots of boys.

In 1955 my brother was overseas with the RAF when he was killed. It broke my mother's heart and she never recovered. We couldn't even bury him and say goodbye. Her hair fell out and never grew back again. By this time I was the only one at home and my parents' grief was huge and I simply couldn't make a dent in it. They couldn't comfort each other either and I would hear them crying separately in the house. They were broken people for a long time. My mother became agoraphobic and had no friends or life beyond the house and my father. She disapproved of me even more by then and would spend as little money on me as possible. We didn't have a relationship at all. She began to drink. Looking back, she must have been so strong because the house continued to be run, food appeared on plates and we never saw her housekeeping standards slip.

After I left home I maintained only a dutiful contact with my mother. She hated my husband and our visits were horrific. When I had my two children she wasn't there at all for motherly guidance or support. At one stage in my life I was poverty stricken, struggling to bring up my son virtually on my own. She never offered to help me. It was a case of having made my own bed and having to lie in it.

When my daughter was born my mother took an instant dislike to her and was horrible to her. I think maybe because she reminded her of me. Our phone calls were stilted. My older sister told me once that Mother had said she never knew what to say to me. She nursed my father when he had a stroke in his eighties. She waited on him hand and foot. Then out of the blue, one morning my brother rang me to say Mum had died in her sleep. It was totally unexpected as she had not been ill. I wept bitterly for her after she died. I stopped thinking of her as the person who had disliked me so much and thought of her just as my mum who I had lost. Sometimes I think it was a good thing that we weren't close because I didn't suffer from her loss as much as I could have done.

I work very hard not to be like my mother with my own children. I have tried always to be the sort of mother I would like to have had. I have tried to be a mother, a teacher and, as they got older, a friend. I think my children like me and like spending time with me. It makes me feel very grateful. My mother never gave me anything – I always felt she kept it for herself. So I have tried to give of myself to my children and to be generous with them. I listen to them as best as I can and I talk with them. That didn't happen in my childhood; maybe it was a generation thing. I never told my mother anything personal. I only knew about periods because my father told me after I'd been in bed for three days in total panic. When my daughter started her period we had a big celebration.

As mothers grow older the question of their care inevitably arises for their families. Depending on background and childhood experience the reactions can be very different. Sally (47) told me:

My mother and I have always had a strained relationship. I was the youngest of three girls and my mother used to say that she wished she had had sons. My dad was a quiet, artistic man. My mother ran the house and the family, and Dad was in the background, going along with her. She was a very small woman in stature, but we used to say that she made up for it in personality. She had been the youngest of three daughters as well and I think she thought I would be like her. I used to fight this when I was young. She was not a tactile woman at all and never told us that she loved us. I missed that when I was a child, but didn't really realise how much until later on in life.

I suppose that my parents were from that between-the-wars generation when life was very tough. They were old-fashioned parents and our emotional life wasn't important or relevant to them. I wasn't very academic, unlike my sisters, but I did pass the eleven-plus and get into grammar school. I remember my mother's only response to the news was to express surprise and assume it 'must have been a bad year' if I'd managed to get in. She undermined me all the time. We never used to argue because she just wouldn't let you argue with her – she always had the last word and that was that.

I didn't do particularly well at the grammar school but I'd always known I wanted to work with young children. Eventually I got a place at a nanny college a long way from home. I was so relieved to get away from home! My mother couldn't see why anyone would want to look after someone else's children. But the minute I walked through the door of the college, I felt at home immediately. I loved my course and was even Student of the Year once. My mother never said 'well done' or expressed any pride in anything I achieved. I wrote home dutifully every week because that was what I thought you were supposed to do. I was only 19, so I went home for holidays. I remember being quite homesick and not wanting to leave sometimes. I was very close to my dad in my late teens and I missed him a lot.

After my career took off I worked for all sorts of families, including ones with very grand houses and glamorous lifestyles. I suppose I moved further away from my mother's own circle of experience and so the distance continued to grow up. I've gone through periods of not seeing my parents very frequently and of spending Christmases apart, etc. My two sisters have families of their own and live some distance away. In our own way we have each had to cope with the lack of affection and love we felt from our mother as children.

My parents are now both 84 and have been married for 58 years. My mother is a stoical Scot and had been very fit and healthy until she was 81 when she became diabetic. My dad willingly took over all the cooking and shopping to manage her diet and look after her. She then had a fall and, after refusing to go to the doctor for four days, she was finally X-rayed and shown to have crushed her spine and be suffering from osteoporosis. Her back will never mend and she has trouble walking now even though she wants to. My dad does everything for her. He is very healthy and seems to cope. Once a year my sisters and I get together to take over his caring responsibilities and send him off for a holiday.

It's very sad really because I see my mother regularly – I live the nearest to them and it's me who is there for emergencies – and yet I never feel I belong to her. I see her only out of a sense of duty. I do feel that I belong to my dad, as we are still close. I went through so many years of hearing hurtful things from her and I feel it's just too late now to make up for it. She asked me recently to hug her. I did as she asked, but I really didn't want to. I don't think she has any concept of what my sisters and I went through and what we missed out on. There was such a cool atmosphere at home. I never once went to her with a problem. I see my sisters enjoying a close relationship with their children and I have seen the mothers I've worked for bonding with their children. I feel envious at times when I see close mother-daughter relationships. As I never had my own children, there was no chance we could ever have 're-bonded' as mothers and daughters can do.

I know she won't be around for ever and if the time came when my dad wasn't around to care for her, she wouldn't be able to live alone but I know that I would never be able to look after her in my home. Her constant criticism, lack of gratitude or praise would drive me round the bend in 24 hours.

My partner and I live partially in Greece now. It's a very family-oriented country and parents there all seem to live near their children. We're planning on moving there permanently soon. When I told my mother she did a double-take and exclaimed that she'd never see me again. She doesn't understand why I'm moving so far from her. Yet although she has never been interested in her family it seems, as she gets older, that she minds more about being close to us. But if we don't do this now the right time will never come and I'm not going to let her reluctance at our move stop me from doing what's right for my partner and me. She was never there for us when we were younger and I know I have shut away a lot of the pain and hurt in her barbed comments. I know I will have to deal with that when she is gone.

Sometimes there is complacency about our mothers. We take them for granted and think they will always be around. I have shared much in this book about my own mother's life and the loss and terrible grief I experienced after she died. I know I am not alone in this suffering and that is as much comfort as we are able to offer one another.

Cheryl (35) told me:

My mother had me when she was only 20. I think I always expected too much of her. I remember being really upset when I was about eight because she was the only mum who came to the school gates wearing flared trousers, platforms and with her long dark hair in bunches. The 'proper mums' had twin-sets and were driving family cars. My mum couldn't drive and we always walked everywhere. I wish I'd had the courage to be proud of her then but all I could see was how different she was.

I was a difficult teenager. Not that I went wild or anything – on the contrary, I worked hard at school and did well. I was pretty horrible to my mum, as only a 13-year-old can be. My mum had left school at 15 to look after her younger brothers and sisters and bring some money into the very poor family she was part of. Escape came in the form of marriage to Dad and she became a mother when she was little more than a child herself. My education had surpassed my mum's when I was only a teenager. She couldn't help with homework and I didn't have the wisdom to appreciate the things she was good at – like playing games, being fun and making things around the house.

The gap between us grew wider as I left home for university and then work. When I got married and had my first child I realised that I needed her. But by then she was suffering from depression and – I discovered only after her death – alcoholism. She had remarried after an amicable divorce from my dad and seemed to be happy in the new marriage to begin with. My mum was a real free spirit and she had great hopes for her own life, none of which ever seemed to come true for her. My stepfather is a good and kind man but very afraid of the world and I think that when she married him, doors closed for her and she lived a very limited life in the house, beset by all sorts of ailments and illnesses.

She died very suddenly from liver failure when she was

only 55. It was the intensive care nurse who asked me if she had been drinking for long. I was so shocked. I had no idea that she had been so unhappy and so ill. The difficult conversations of the past few years, her reluctance to visit us or to get involved with her grandchildren all made sense suddenly. I sat by her bed and held her hand while she died.

I don't think I will ever get over these things. I thought we had years ahead of us, and plenty of time for our relationship to improve. I imagined caring for her in her old age. When my grandmother was dying, my mum was a totally devoted daughter and she encouraged me to help look after her mother with her. It was the sort of family where you took responsibility for the elderly; there was no question of putting anyone in a home. I remember giving my grandmother a foot massage and pedicure when I was in my teens. Her feet were pretty horrible! The toenails were yellow and curled and she had varicose veins up and down her legs. But my mum insisted that I show her the respect and love she was due and afterwards I remember feeling proud of myself and sure that I would one day care for my own mother in such a way. I've been denied those years and I feel angry and sad about it. There's no hope for recovering our relationship now and no chance left for me to help her or for her to help me.

I have certainly found that there is a tradition among the more working-class families of caring for the generation above. Often these are large families who still live near each other and can share the responsibility of caring. It seems that each generation looks to the one above for guidance on how to cope with the twilight years. The more firm the family's practices, the less questioning takes place over what is 'right'.

Juliette (49) told me about her mother:

My mother is 80 now and was in good health until a few years ago. She had seven children in nine years. She has 21 grandchildren and 14 great-grandchildren and her family has been her whole life. Caring for other people has been everything to her and I know she holds no resentment at all about it. She's remarkable – a serene and very creative person still. She writes poetry and stories for all the children and she helps look after my sister's twins as well as being at the heart of our huge family.

Mum was the eldest daughter of eight. Having lots of children seems to run in our family – I have five of my own! When we were young my dad was offered a job in Australia with assisted passage for the whole family. They turned it down because my mum wouldn't leave her own parents. She felt it was her duty to care for them in old age.

We grew up in frightening poverty. I remember that my dad and uncles used to go out rustling chickens and vegetables just so we could eat. But Mum was tough and very resourceful. She had standards that we had to live up to. She instilled good manners in us all. We were always supposed to be clean and tidy. On Sunday nights we were scrubbed to within an inch of our lives. She would spend the summer holidays knitting jumpers for us to wear to school. I remember waking up every year on the first day back at school. There would be seven sets of school uniforms neatly lined up in piles, with two handmade jumpers for each of us to wear for the year.

As we grew up she never interfered in our lives but she's always been there for all of us. We don't always see eye to eye but we're blood and the importance of that bond has been at the centre of my life. I hope I'm passing it on to my five children. I have taken many of my mum's values into my own family.

I think we were all brought up to support each other, in tough times and good times. We lost two of my brothers in the last few years and it's since then that my mother's health has deteriorated. One brother was tragically killed when he was 37. She's never got over this. My other brother was 42 and died from AIDS. His death took a whole year. In the final six months of his life he took over the top floor of my parents' house. We all came round and transformed it into the most beautiful sitting room/bedroom for him. We shared caring for him and most of us saw him every day. He died with his family around him, showering him with their love and care.

I know my mother is now approaching the time when she will need to be cared for and nursed. Even though my youngest child is still only eight I won't find this a burden or an unwelcome responsibility. We will do what we always do and share the care between us. I don't understand any other way.

As much as women ask themselves are they good mothers, when their own mothers reach the end of their lives, the question arises 'Am I good daughter?' There is an assumption that we should care for our mothers as they cared for us when we were children. These women were often homemakers with no life outside the home or local community. Many women today have memories of mothers who were always there when they got home from school or who had careers in a very low-level way compared to what women enjoy now. The options of combining work and motherhood didn't always exist and so the sense of duty towards one's elderly parent can feel quite automatic.

An earlier chapter of this book was devoted to mothers as best friend figures. I heard from many women about the closeness that is possible. Having been intensely close to my own mother, I found these stories very moving and uplifting. But some women have felt distant from their mothers, as Cheryl explained above, and when death takes place the burden of guilt and regret can be overwhelming. In some families mothers have not been 'good' and have caused their children terrible suffering. When old age looms there can be burdens of blame, resentment and anger to bear as well as the bewildering sense of responsibility and care.

Sophie (45) has five children aged between 19 and 9. She told me about her mother and her childhood:

My mother had a very traumatic childhood. She was born in Poland and helped her mother care for her three brothers. Just before the Second World War broke out, my mother's mother hanged herself. Her father quickly remarried a German woman. When my mother reached the age of 15 her stepmother was very threatened by her emerging sexuality and effectively threw my mother out of the family home. She had to leave behind the brothers she adored, one of whom was still a toddler, and she found herself in a labour camp with all its horrors of poverty and abuse.

By the age of 30 my mother was in England, married to a man twice her age, but settled and secure. She gave birth to me and, as a result, felt a great need to try and trace her family whom she had not seen for 15 years. Through the Red Cross she found them living in Germany. Perhaps understandably, this reunion combined with my birth caused a massive mental breakdown. She was hospitalised for two years. My dad was 60 at this point and couldn't raise a child on his own. A woman in our road became my childminder and looked after me. She was having an affair outside her marriage and I became a substitute child for her and her boyfriend. When their relationship became official, they were appointed my godparents by my dad and she wanted me to call her 'Mummy'. When I was two my mother came home and I had to learn to call her Mummy and get to know her.

A few normal years passed but when I reached 11 my mother had another breakdown and was hospitalised. My childminder neighbour had left the street but my godfather was still there and took over caring for me as my dad was almost 70 by then. He abused me for two years.

When Mum came out of hospital again she was physically present but mentally a long way from me or anything. I was very angry with her, of course. I struggled through my teens, hating myself and behaving in a fairly destructive way. I cared completely for both my parents. I did all the washing and the cooking and towards the end of my dad's life I had to feed him.

School was my escape. I was given some counselling there which helped enormously. Academically I did very well, against all the odds. I had some wonderful teachers who took me to galleries and to the theatre. After my father died, I escaped to university. He had left me a house and I went to live in it and study locally for a degree in English and Religious Studies. I left my mother alone in London and was desperately relieved to get away from the depressing and unhappy house.

I married very young, at 19, and was divorced by 21. I then met a very charismatic older man. My father had just died and I was drawn to him because he was more mature than other men I knew. He had a very glamorous lifestyle with plenty of money. He was also an alcoholic and a drug addict. I had two daughters by him and we all moved away to the countryside. It should have been perfect. All I wanted was a happy house and a family. But he drank and drank and then became violent. I could never call on my mother for help as she was so helpless herself. Eventually, when my daughters were aged two and three, I realised I couldn't let them see their father treating me like this any more and with the help of friends I found a solicitor and tried to get him out of my home and my life.

He still sees his daughters and they don't see his nasty side at all, which is hard for me. I didn't cope very well as a single parent. Life was very tough and I threw myself into a series of hopeless relationships, looking for security and love in all the wrong places. And then I met Luke. He was the same age as me and we quickly married. We had three more children one after the other and life has become easier. My teenage daughters are now going quite wild. One wants to spend her gap year as a lap dancer! I wonder all the time whether I have been a good or a bad mother. Because of the abuse I suffered I have never been able to consider childcare for any of my children and I have been home for them full-time from the start. It has sometimes been boring and at times I have felt that I have almost had to lobotomise myself to cope with the dreary daily grind of providing meals, washing and cleaning.

My mother is now in her eighties. She has been very generous financially to us and I see her often. She moved to the country to live near us some years ago. She enjoyed being a grandmother when she was fit and helped me a great deal. Now she is blind and virtually deaf. She is fiercely independent and lives alone with some help from social services and from me. I'm an only child and I can't walk away from her. She is still very depressing company and I can only visit her when I am feeling buoyant and positive. She talks about death a lot. I know that I won't be able to nurse her myself if she becomes ill enough to need that. I have used up all my years of caring already, looking after her when I was a teenager and trying to be a good mother to my own five children.

Regardless of how you get on with your mother, life comes full circle and one day you will most likely become the parent to an ill or dying, elderly mum or dad. As a mother of young children you love them, care for them, but while doing so you want to protect them from the hurt life throws at them as you prepare them for the life they have ahead.

When the role inevitably reverses, the main difference is that the person you are caring for has no life ahead of them in which you will hopefully get to share and from which you may take pleasure. Bestselling children's book author Jill Murphy said in a *Sunday Times* article (October 2005) about her much-loved mother's decline into senility: 'It was like being a mother to a very small child, but instead of the child growing up there was this terrible ending.' You bring up your children knowing they are more than likely to outlive you. With a parent you expect to witness their death and this can make caring for them a long and painful process.

In the last 10–15 years there has been a shift towards women having their babies later and later. This means it is becoming increasingly common for a mother to be nearing the end of raising her own children, getting them off to college or jobs when her own parents demand those same levels of care and help. The period of life many women look forward to – the end of parenting responsibilities and time to enjoy some freedom and, eventually, the grandchildren – is often sacri-ficed these days to a whole new kind of parenting.

Let's not forget either that the baby a mother cares for is an object of intense beauty. A child is perfect in his mother's eyes. His skin, his hair, his smile are all brand new and their beauty gives daily pleasure. Only a mother knows the delight of watching their child grow up. When you are caring for an elderly person they are far from beautiful and what you are witnessing is a decline. In my earliest memory of my mother in that storm when we went to see my father, her beautiful glossy black hair was plastered to her face by the rain and the tears.

In my last memory of her she had no hair at all. Her eyes, which were so bright and clear on that wet night, were clouded with pain at the end of her life. To watch the approach of death in someone you care so deeply about is to face your own mortality. It is to be reluctantly moved up the next rung on the ladder of life and the next step towards your own death.

When life goes full circle and you become the mother to your mother, you may love her and care for her in a similar way to the way you care for your children and you want to protect her in the same way. But deep down you are carrying the sadness in your heart that you are preparing her for death. Depending on your beliefs, it may be eternal life, a life that is more beautiful and joyful than anything that life on earth can bring. But whatever your beliefs, the one sadness for those of us who were fortunate enough to have a close relationship with our mother is that death means the end of that relationship as we know it.

Conclusion

Well, where does this leave us as we reflect on what makes a 'good' or a 'bad' mother? The answer is, of course, that there is no answer. I hope that the many and varied voices I have included here will illustrate what I found during the writing of this book: that everyone has a story and everyone's story is unique. We have no right to sit in judgement on one another, and it makes no sense to judge ourselves.

For mothers today the world has many, many answers. They shout at you from the bookshelves and the magazine racks; from the television and the radio; from your mother, your grandmother, your friends and the old lady on the bus. Some opinions will be right for you and some won't.

Rather than squabbling among ourselves about whether we breast-feed to six months or one year; whether we use brown rice or white rice and whether raising your left eyebrow at your baby will make it lose its confidence, we ought to be reaching out to each other and to the children in our society who are truly neglected and uncared for. We ought to be helping the mothers who don't have the education or the support and information to make choices. We ought to be working together to put pressure on the government, the media and employers to improve the lives of mothers and children everywhere.

You will have, I hope, a lifetime to be a mother to your child. Some mothers are superb with tiny babies but less successful with older children. Some are the opposite and their relationship with their children flourishes as a more grown-up stage is reached. Most mothers do as my mother did – their best with what they have. You can't expect to be perfect, although I know how hard most mothers want to be perfect. The loved child, whether breast- or bottle-fed, attachment or routine, will always be happier than the unloved.

There is such innocence and joy in the times when thoughts of twilight years are far ahead in the future. The joys and innocence of childhood are there to be nurtured by mothers. Mothers, however they choose to bring up their children, should be united in one thing: that the hand that rocks the cradle is the hand that rules the world. Instead of competing and arguing the small issues, we should be united in making the world a better place for all children to grow up in. They are our future and children live what they learn. Let us live in harmony together and agree to disagree on some aspects of motherhood, but stand united on the important ones. Let us make life on earth beautiful and joyful for all mothers and their children. This can only be done by mutual respect and understanding.

References

Biddulph, Steve, *Raising Boys*, HarperCollins (2003)

Dick, Diana, *Yesterday's Babies*, The Bodley Head (1987)

Enright, Anne, *Making Babies: Stumbling into Motherhood*, Cape (2001)

Figes, Kate, *Life after Birth*, Penguin (2000)

Hakim, Dr Catherine, *Work-Lifestyle Choices in the 21st Century: Preference Theory*, Oxford University Press (2000)

Helle, Samuli, (University of Turku), Virpi Lummaa (Cambridge University), Jukka Jokela (University of Oulu), *Sons Reduced Maternal Longevity in Pre-Industrial Humans*, 2002. Contact press and publications office, University of Cambridge

Hill, Amelia, 'The £3bn cost of bringing up an Alpha child', *The Observer*, Sunday 3 April 2005

Hunt, Jan, M.Sc., *Empathetic Grandparenting*, The Natural Child Project, www.naturalchild.com

King, Professor Michael, and Dr Eamonn McKeown, *Mental health and social wellbeing of gay men, lesbians and bisexuals in England and Wales*, Mind (2003)

Lee, Dr Ellie, and Professor Frank Furedi, *Mothers' experience of, and attitudes to, using infant formula in the early months*, School of Social Policy, Sociology and Social Research, University of Kent (June 2005)

Liedloff, Jean, *The Continuum Concept*, 2nd edn, Arkana (1989)

Murphy, Jill, 'Parenting: the longest goodbye', in conversation with Amanda Craig, *The Sunday Times*, 16 October 2005

Parsons, Rob, *The Sixty Minute Mother*, Hodder (2000)

Websites

www.futurefoundation.net

The National Survey of Sexual Attitudes and Lifestyle, available at www.natcen.ac.uk

Organisations

The Institute for the Study of Children, Families and Social Issues, Birkbeck, University of London, 7 Bedford Square, London, WC1B 3RA, www.iscfsi.bbk.ac.uk

ALSO BY GINA FORD
AVAILABLE FROM VERMILION

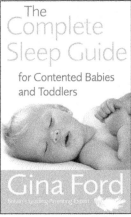

ALSO BY GINA FORD
AVAILABLE FROM VERMILION

Also by

Coming soon from
Random House Children's Books

AUTUMN 06

Gina Ford's Bedtime Songs for
Contented Little Babies (£9.99)

A beautiful book of songs and lullabies that will help soothe your baby to sleep. Includes a CD containing over 30 minutes of tranquil songs and music, just right for helping your baby drift off at sleeptime.

SPRING 07

Gina Ford's Books for
Contented Babies and Toddlers (£4.99)

Perfect for little hands, these bright lift-the-flap board books encourage learning through play. Children will love lifting the sturdy flaps to see what happens next!

Ella and Tom: Going on a Picnic

Ella and Tom: Sleepy Time

These feely board books are ideal for babies and parents to share. The vibrant pictures and different textures make learning fun!

Ella and Tom: Let's Play

Ella and Tom: On the Farm